EARTH'S BIOMES

Ecology and Biodiversity

Encyclopedia Kids | Science Grade 7 | Children's Environment Books

BABY PROFESSOR
EDUCATION KIDS

First Edition, 2020

Published in the United States by Speedy Publishing LLC, 40 E Main Street, Newark, Delaware 19711 USA.

© 2020 Baby Professor Books, an imprint of Speedy Publishing LLC

All rights reserved.

Without limiting the rights under the copyright reserved above, no part of this publication may be reproduced, stored in or introduced into a retrieval system, or transmitted, in any form, or by any means (electronic, mechanical, photocopying, recording, or otherwise), without the prior written permission of the copyright owner.

All images in this book have been reproduced with the knowledge and prior consent of the artists concerned, and no responsibility is accepted by producer, publisher, or printer for any infringement of copyright or otherwise arising from the contents of this publication.

Baby Professor Books are available at special discounts when purchased in bulk for industrial and sales-promotional use. For details contact our Special Sales Team at Speedy Publishing LLC, 40 E Main Street, Newark, Delaware 19711 USA. Telephone (888) 248-4521 Fax: (210) 519-4043.

10 9 8 7 6 * 5 4 3 2 1

Print Edition: 9781541949553
Digital Edition: 9781541951358
Hardcover Edition: 9781541975958

See the world in pictures. Build your knowledge in style.
www.speedypublishing.com

TABLE OF CONTENTS

Dividing the Planet into Biomes 7
How Many Biomes Are There? 11
A World of Biomes 15
The Temperate Forest 19
Plants and Animals in a Temperate Forest 25
The Desert Biome 33
Plants and Animals of the Desert Biome 39
The Tropical Rainforest 45
Plants and Animals of the Tropical Rainforest 49
The Grassland Biome 53
Plants and Animals of the Grassland 57
The Tundra Biome 63
Plants and Animals of the Tundra 67
The Savanna Biome 71
Plants and Animals of the Savanna 75
The Taiga Biome 81
Plants and Animals of the Taiga Biome 85
The Freshwater Biome 89
Plants and Animals of the Freshwater Biome 91
The Marine Biome 95
The Plants and Animals of the Marine Biome 99
Summary 102

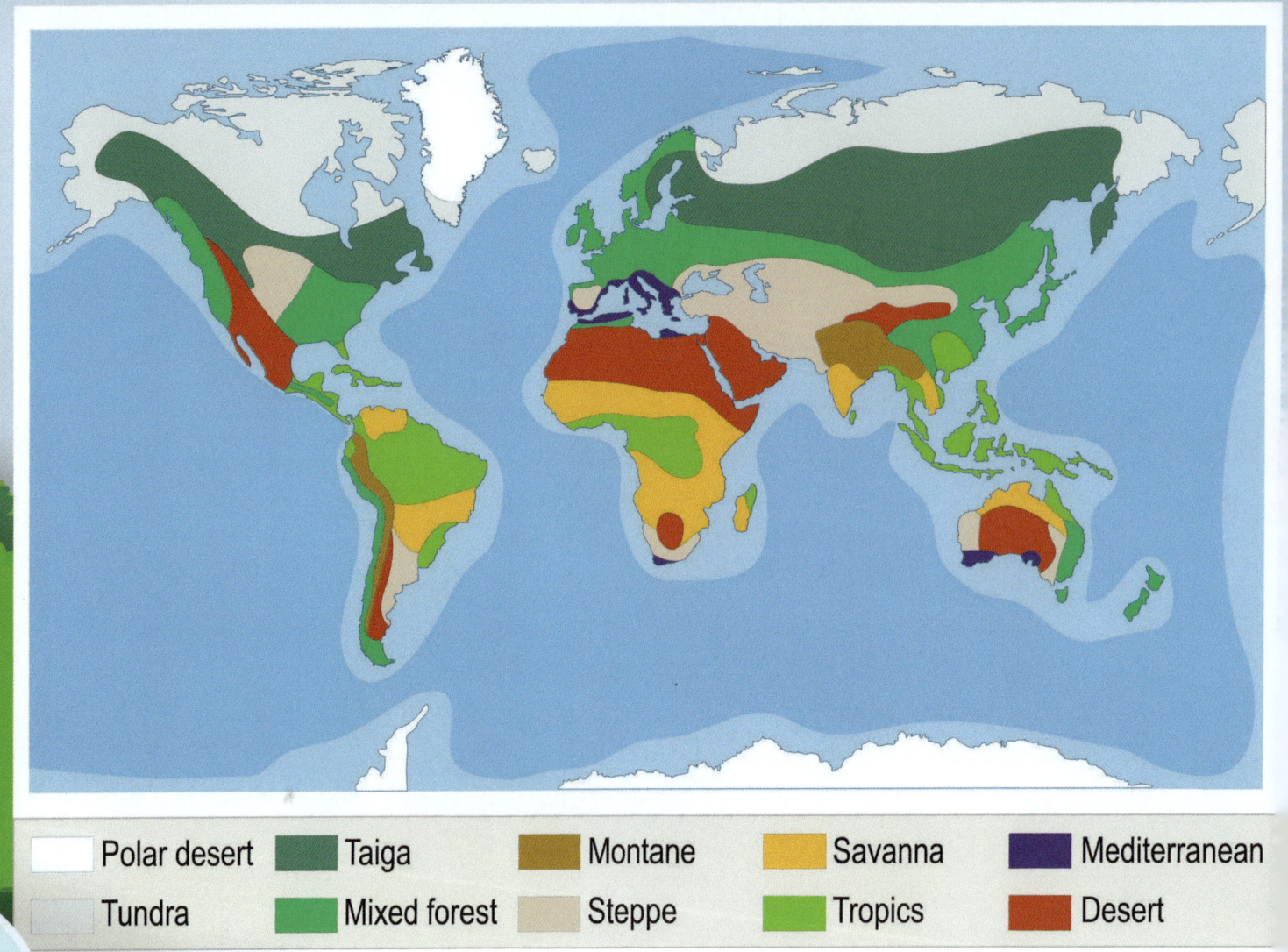

Polar desert | Taiga | Montane | Savanna | Mediterranean
Tundra | Mixed forest | Steppe | Tropics | Desert

THE MAIN BIOMES IN THE WORLD

The Earth is a diverse planet. There are many different places, each with their own climate, plants, and geographical features. Scientists call these biomes. A biome is defined as a vast, naturally occurring community of plants and animals. In this book, we will look at nine of the major biomes on Earth, the distinguishing characteristics of each one, as well as the living things that call these biomes home. Let's get started.

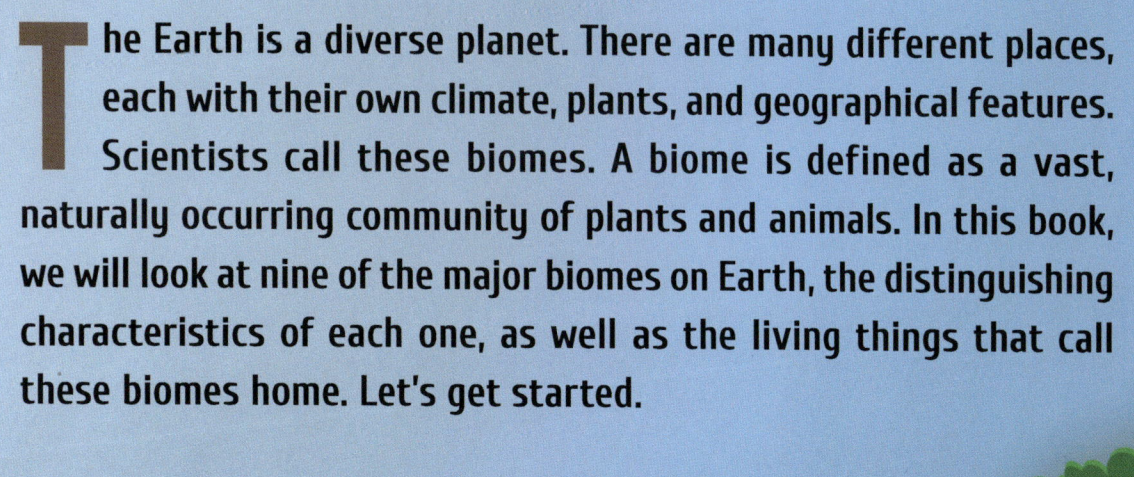

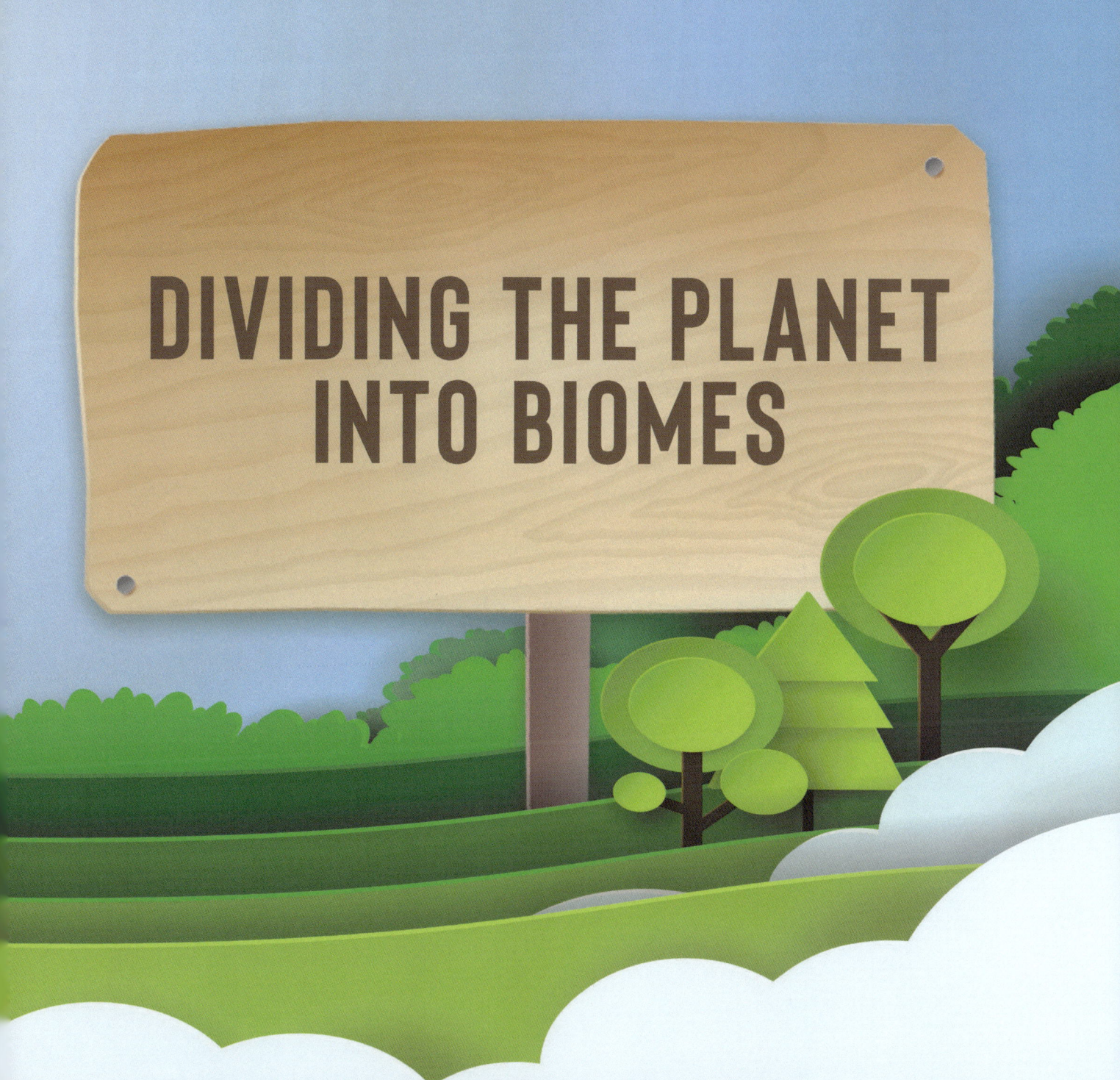

FREDERICK EDWARD CLEMENTS

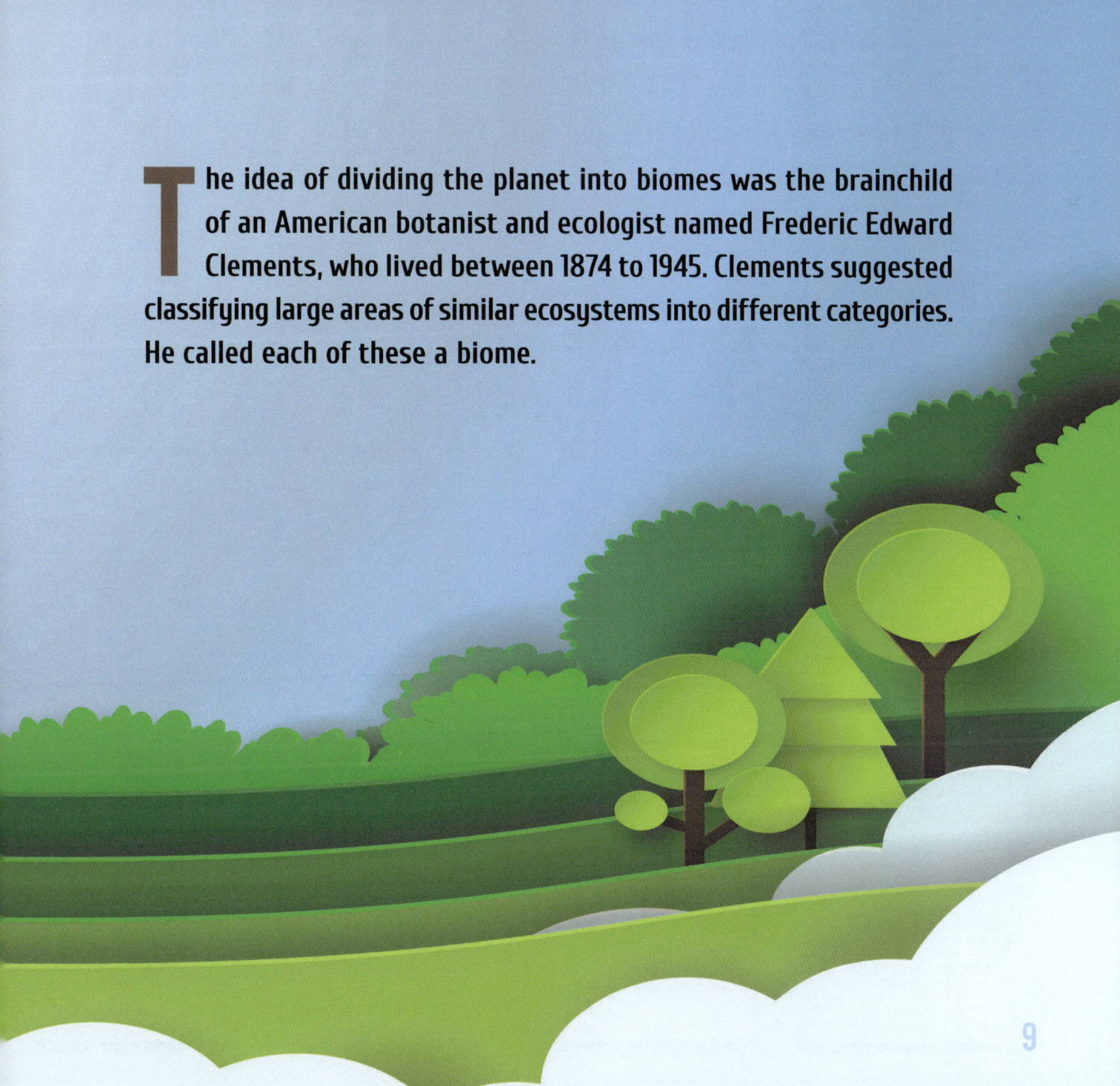

The idea of dividing the planet into biomes was the brainchild of an American botanist and ecologist named Frederic Edward Clements, who lived between 1874 to 1945. Clements suggested classifying large areas of similar ecosystems into different categories. He called each of these a biome.

In the decades after Clements first divided the Earth into different biomes, the term has been refined to include the geography, climate, and plant life in each area. The benefit of grouping similar areas into the same biome helps scientists to study and discuss how these regions are similar despite their different locations.

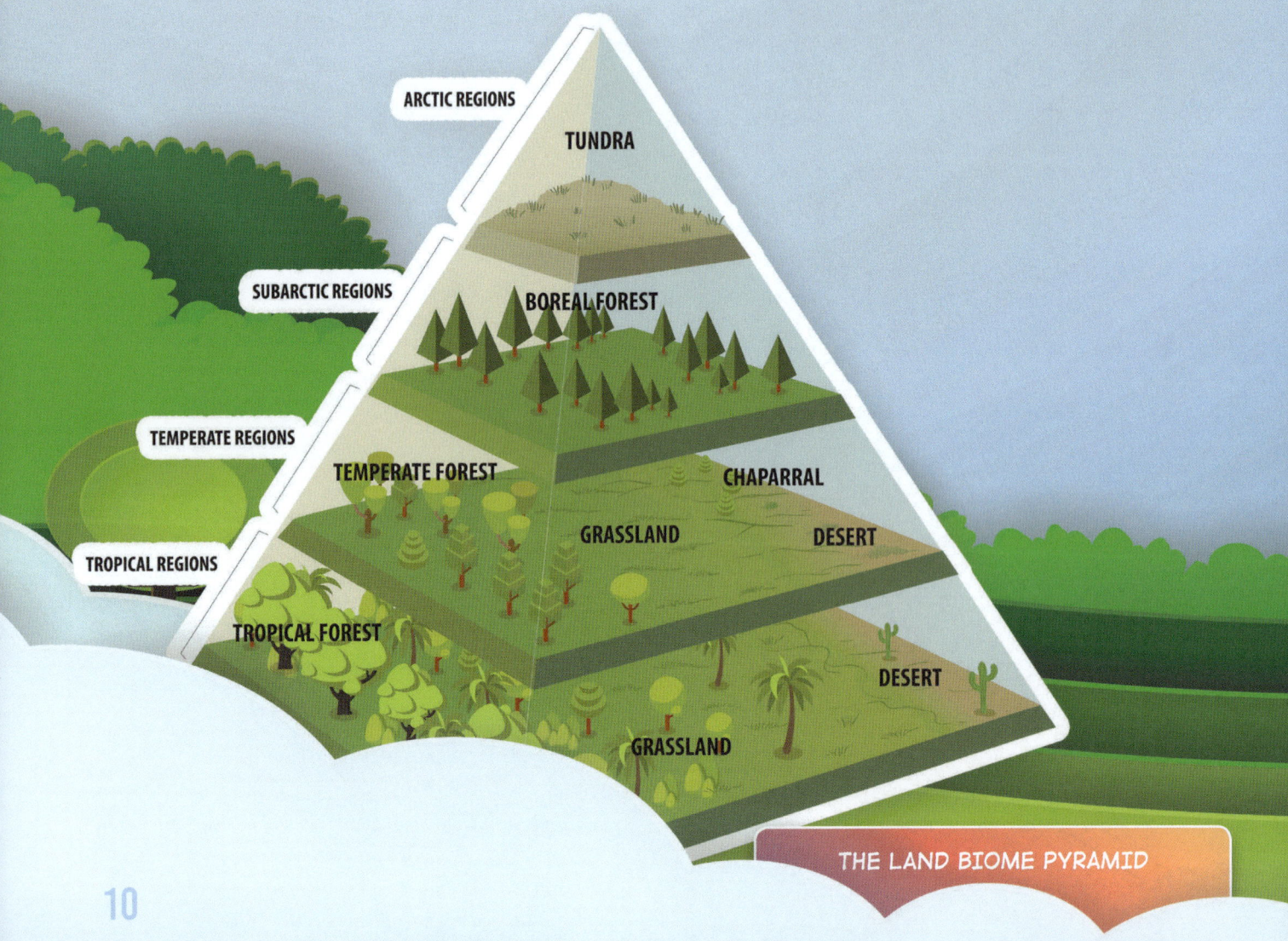

THE LAND BIOME PYRAMID

Depending on who you ask, you will get different answers to the question of how many biomes there are on Earth. You may hear that there are as few as five biomes or as many as twenty. Some biologists, for example, believe that all forest ecosystems should be considered the same biome, yet there are other scientists who think that the forest ecosystem should be divided even more, based on climate because there are big differences between different types of forests.

Altitudinal Zonation

- Ice And Snow
- Tundra
- Needleleaf Forest
- Temperature Deciduous Forest
- Tropical Rain Forest

Latitudinal Zonation

Broadleaf Evergreen Forest | Tropical Grassland | Desert | Desert Scrub | Chaparral | Temperate Grassland | Deciduous Forest | Mixed Forest | Coniferous Forest | Tundra | Ice Cap

THE MAIN BIOMES ILLUSTRATED IN RELATION TO LATITUDE AND CLIMATE.

A tropical rainforest like the Amazon, they argue, is totally different than a temperate[1] forest with pine trees, deer, and bears. Identifying where one biome ends and another one starts can be tricky. In many cases, there are some overlaps. Some plants and animals, for example, can live in more than one biome.

1   Temperate – Not subject to prolonged extremes of hot or cold temperatures.

AMAZON RAINFOREST IN BRAZIL

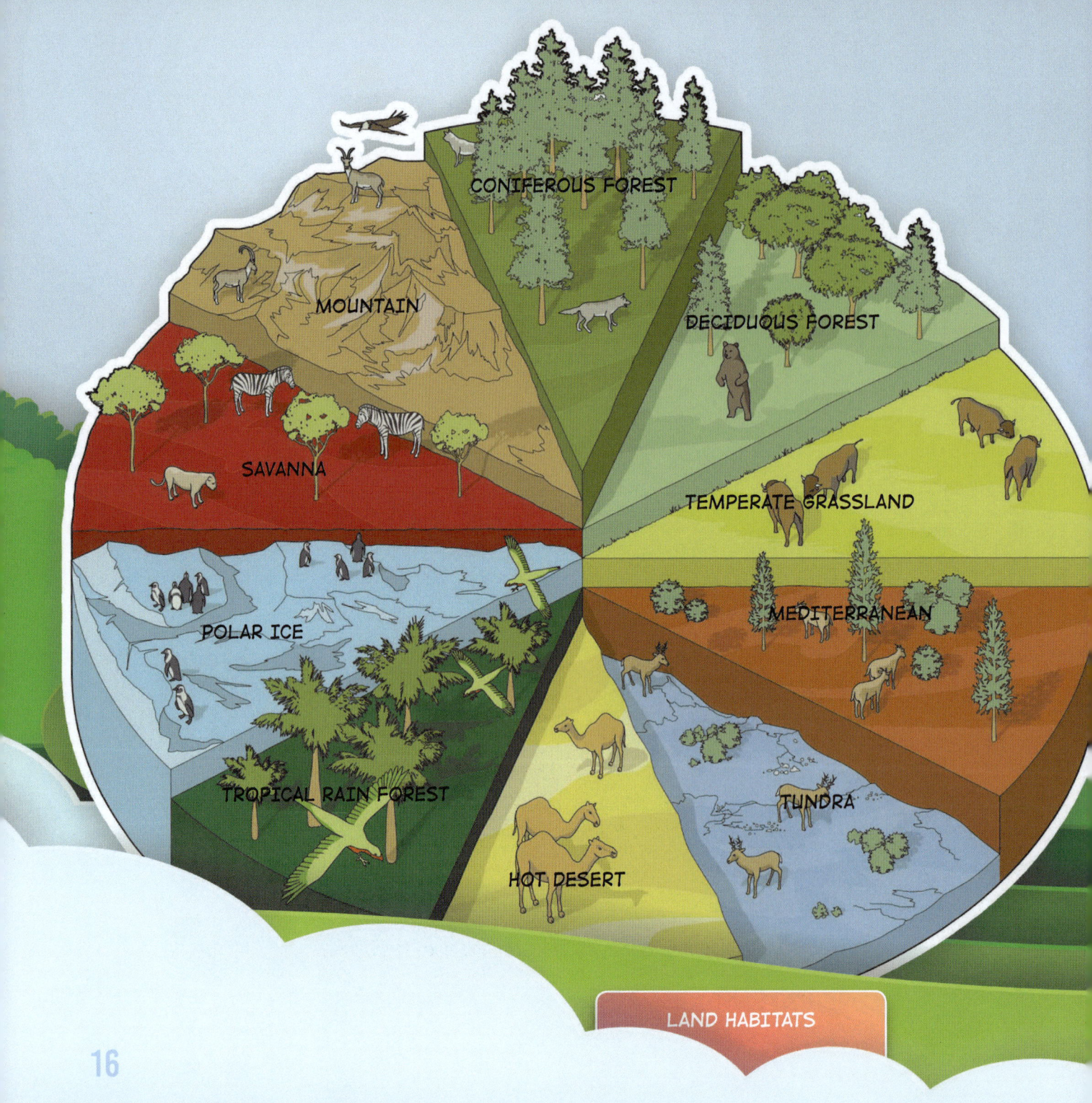
LAND HABITATS

No matter if you divide the planet into five biomes or twenty, there will be ways to further divide and classify each biome into smaller and smaller subcategories that are different from each other. This is a testament to the great diversity of planet Earth and the uniqueness of individual places. For the purpose of this book, however, we will focus in on biomes in the broad sense of the term. In the following sections, we will discuss nine different biomes and explain what makes each one of them special.

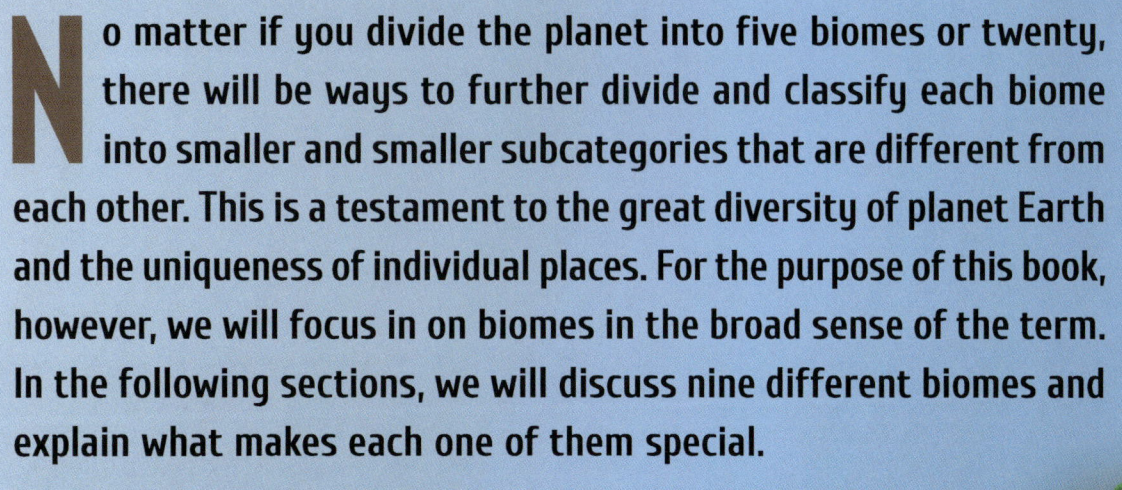

Temperate forests are most often found in the Northern Hemisphere, or the lands located above the Equator[2]. You will find temperate forests in parts of Europe, in the eastern United States and Canada, and in Eastern Asia, to name a few.

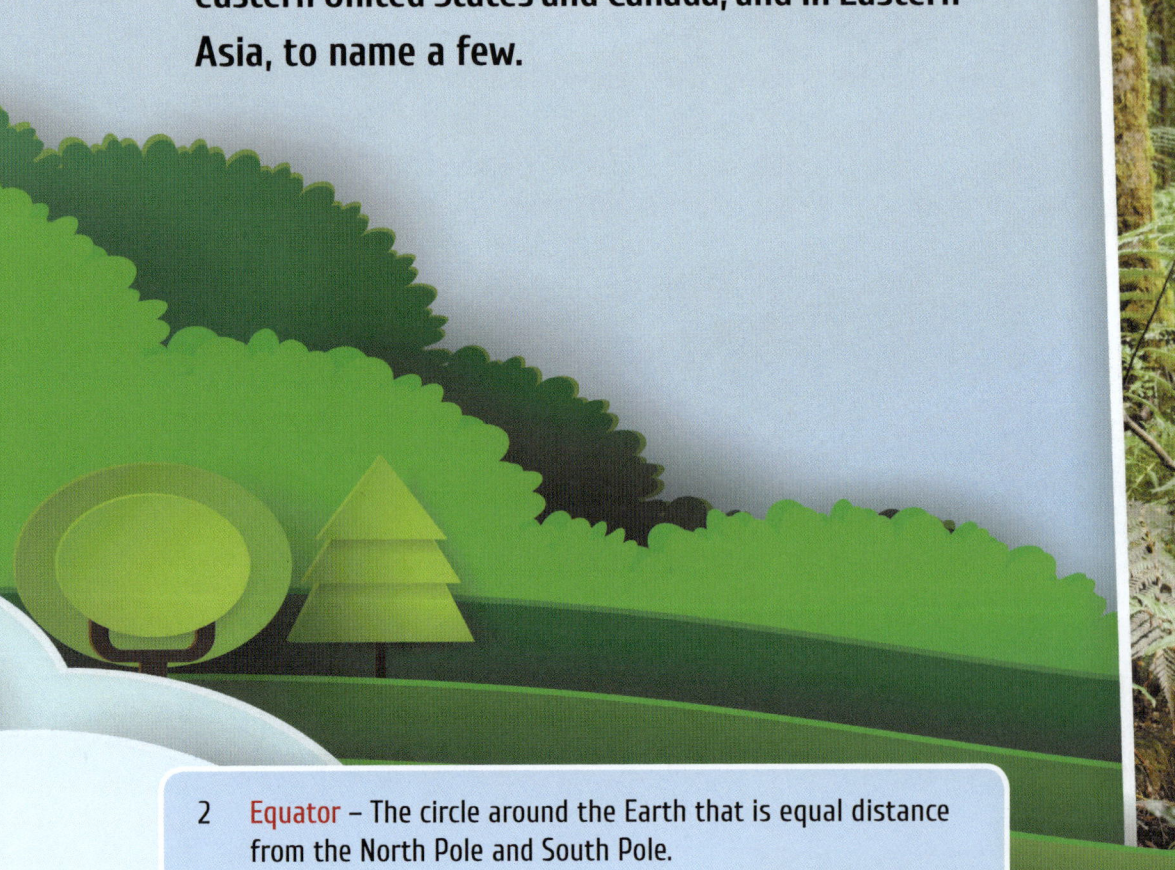

2   Equator – The circle around the Earth that is equal distance from the North Pole and South Pole.

TEMPERATE RAINFOREST IN YARRA RANGES, VICTORIA, AUSTRALIA

TEMPERATE FORESTS CAN GET AS COLD AS TWENTY BELOW ZERO IN THE WINTERTIME.

An important feature of the temperate forest is that the biome experiences four distinct seasons—a wet Spring, a warm and humid Summer, a cool Autumn, and a cold, snowy Winter. In the Summer months, a temperate forest can see temperatures climb into the upper eighties and lower nineties. In the Wintertime, it can get as cold as twenty below zero. On average, a temperate forest will receive between 25 and 60 inches of precipitation[3]—in the form of either rain or snow—per year.

3   Precipitation – Any type of water falling from the atmosphere, including rain, snow, hail, etc.

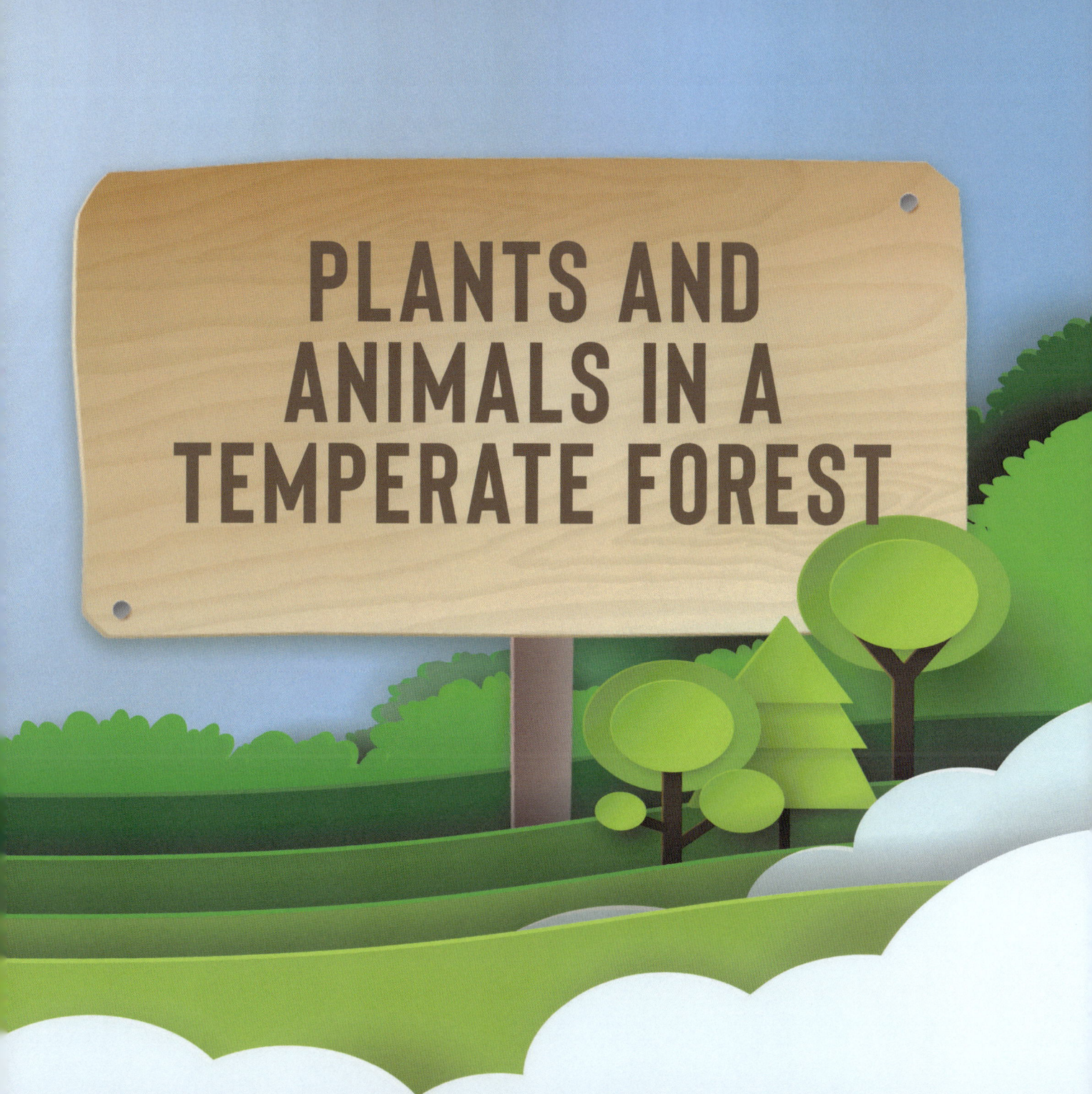

Plants and Animals in a Temperate Forest

Temperate forests are home to deciduous trees – trees that drop their leaves every Autumn and regrow new leaves in the Spring. Oaks, maples, walnuts, hickory, poplars, and cherry trees are common in a temperate forest.

HICKORY TREES

POPLAR TREES

MAPLE TREES

WALNUT TREES

CERRY TREES

OAK TREES

27

In addition to these, you will find moss and lichen[4] in temperate forests, as well as wildflowers, like jack in the pulpits and trilliums; bramble[5] vines, like huckleberries and blackberries; shrubs, like dogwoods and redbuds; and low-lying plants, like ferns and grasses.

4   Lichen – A low growing plant organism that is similar to moss and algae.
5   Bramble – A prickly shrub.

A wide range of animals, from insects to mammals and birds to reptiles, make their home in the temperate forest biome. Squirrels, raccoons, deer, coyotes, mountain lions, snakes, eagles, hawks, robins, beetles, ticks, mosquitos, and spiders are among the wildlife in this biome.

About one-fifth of the planet's land is classified as a desert biome. The driest of all the regions on Earth, deserts receive very little annual rainfall. On average, a desert biome can expect less than 20 inches of rain each year.

SONORAN DESERT NEAR PHOENIX, ARIZONA

GREAT VICTORIA DESERT IN CENTRAL AUSTRALIA

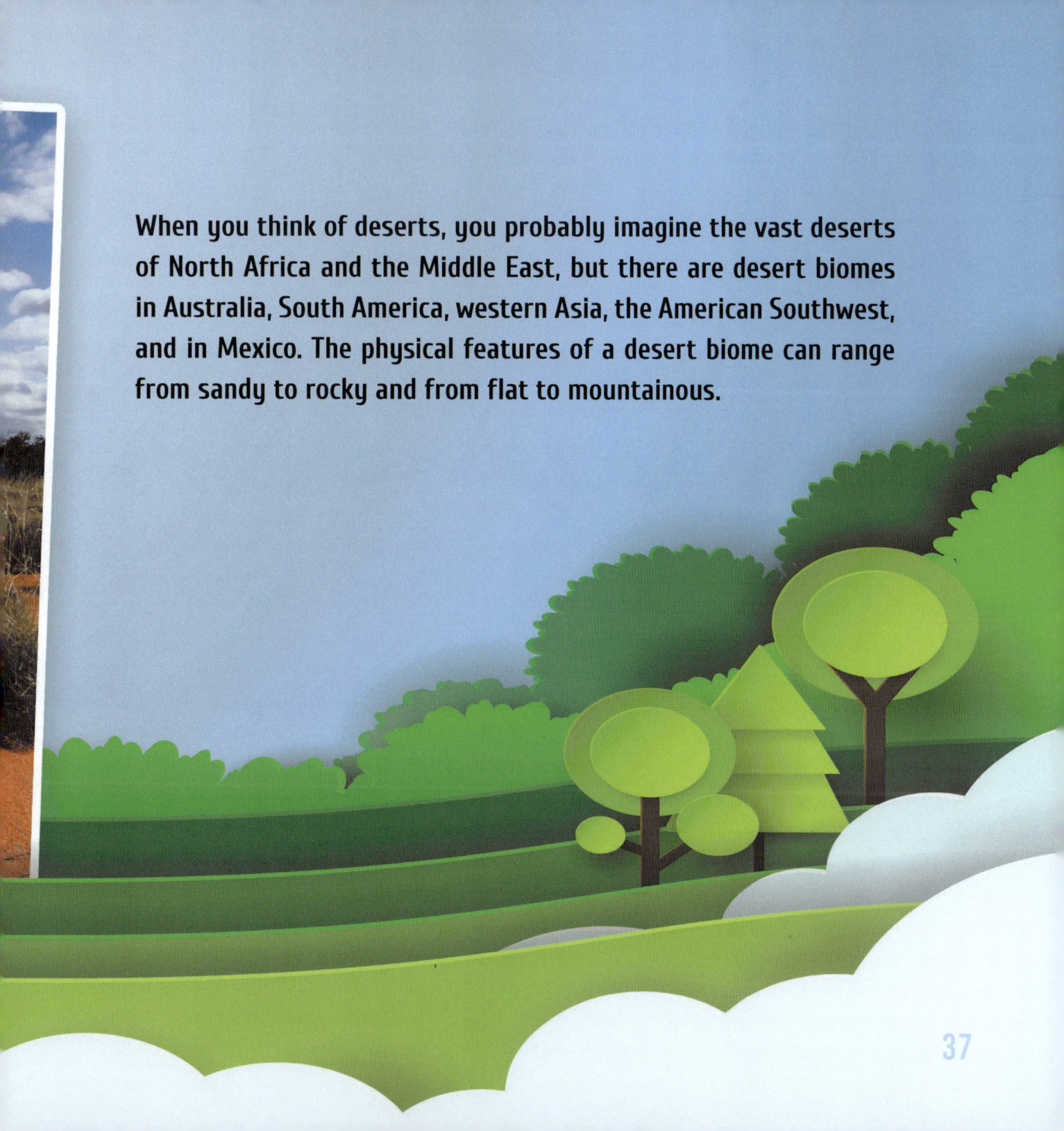

When you think of deserts, you probably imagine the vast deserts of North Africa and the Middle East, but there are desert biomes in Australia, South America, western Asia, the American Southwest, and in Mexico. The physical features of a desert biome can range from sandy to rocky and from flat to mountainous.

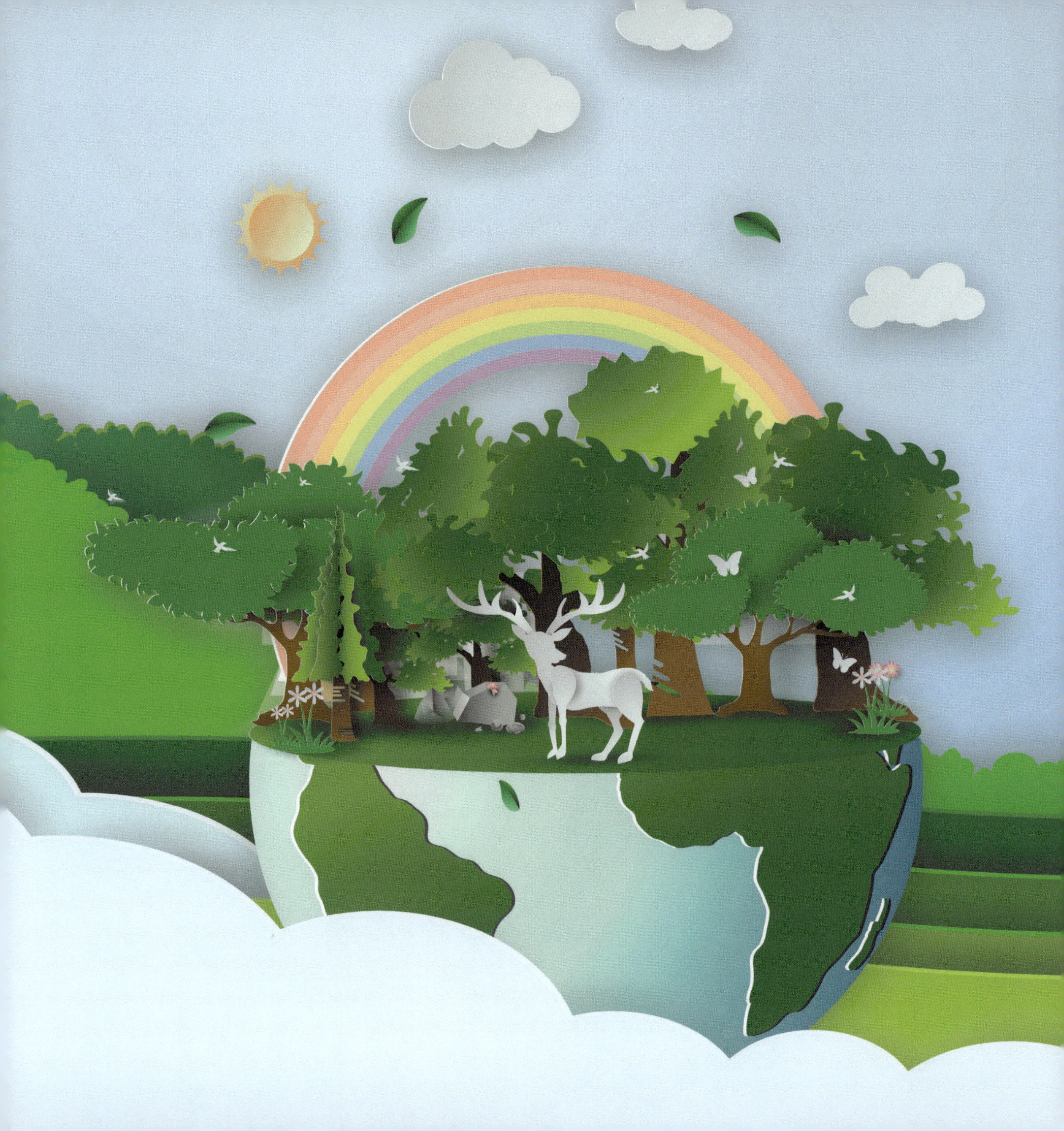

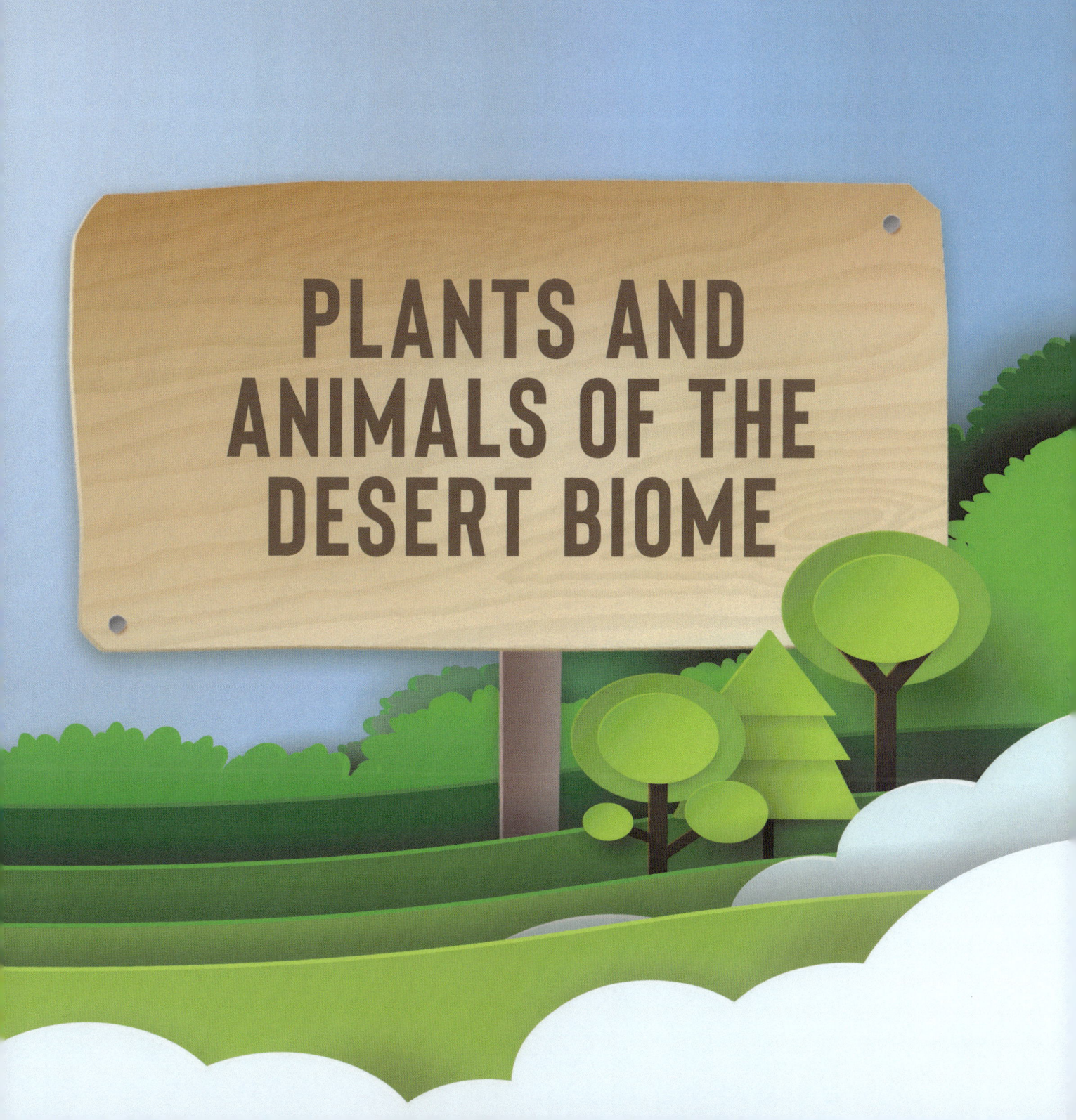

PLANTS AND ANIMALS OF THE DESERT BIOME

Plants native to the desert biomes of the world have adapted to their harsh habitat. They are designed to withstand the drought-like conditions of the region and to conserve the little rainwater that does fall. Trees are often scarce in many desert biomes, but in others, you may find desert willows, Chilean mesquite, and tipu.

WILLOWS

CHILEAN MESQUITE

TIPU

40

Cacti[6] are common in the desert and come in a variety of shapes and sizes from the ground-hugging parodia and Bishop's cap cacti to the towering Saguaro. In addition to cacti, the desert is home to sagebrush, thistle, grasses, creosote bushes, and wildflowers.

| PARODIA | BISHOP'S CAP | SAGUARO |
| SAGEBRUSH | THISTLE | CREOSOTE BUSH |

6   Cacti – The plural form of cactus.

The vegetation in the desert biome provides a food source for the animals that live there, including small rodents, lizards, rabbits, snakes, scorpions, roadrunners, and hawks.

LIZARD	RABBIT	SNAKE
SCORPION	ROADRUNNERS	HAWKS

Coyote, deer, antelope, and meerkat can also be found in the deserts of the world.

COYOTE

DEER

ANTELOPE

MEERKAT

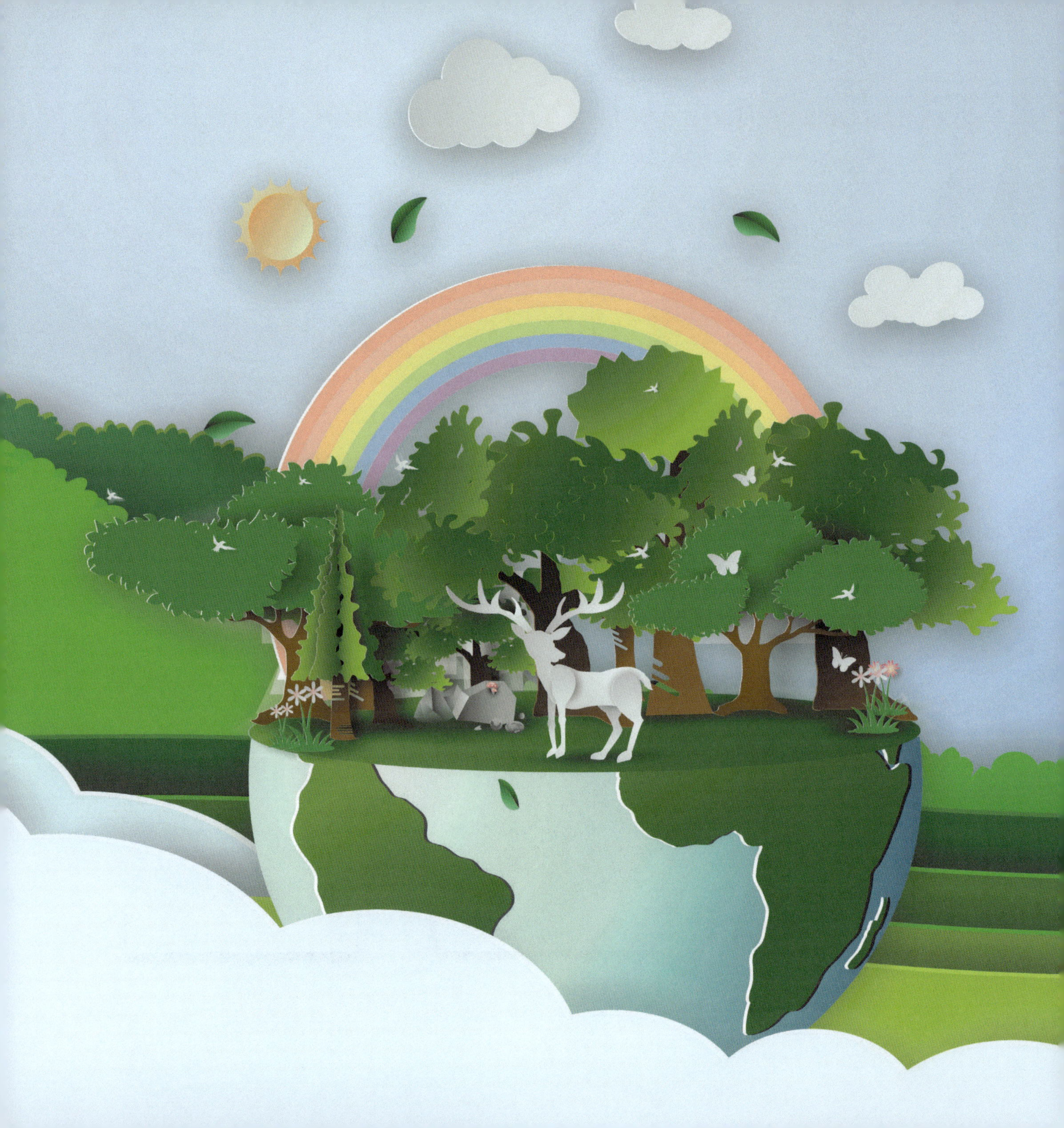

THE TROPICAL RAINFOREST

Even though the tropical rainforest biome only covers about seven-percent of the land on Earth, it is such an important biome that it is often called the "lungs of the planet". There are so many plants and trees in the tropical rainforests that these regions release quite a bit of oxygen into the air. The biggest tropical rainforest biome in the world is the Amazon forest of South America, however there are tropical rainforests in other areas, too.

TROPICAL RAINFOREST, AMAZON YASUNI, ECUADOR

There are tropical rainforests in Equatorial Africa and in the thousands of islands of Indonesia. The tropical rainforest is hot and wet. Temperatures average between 72 and 85-degrees year round and it is not uncommon for this biome to receive as much as 400 inches of rain annually.

BENANG KELAMBU WATERFALL IN THE TROPICAL FOREST AT LOMBOK, INDONESIA

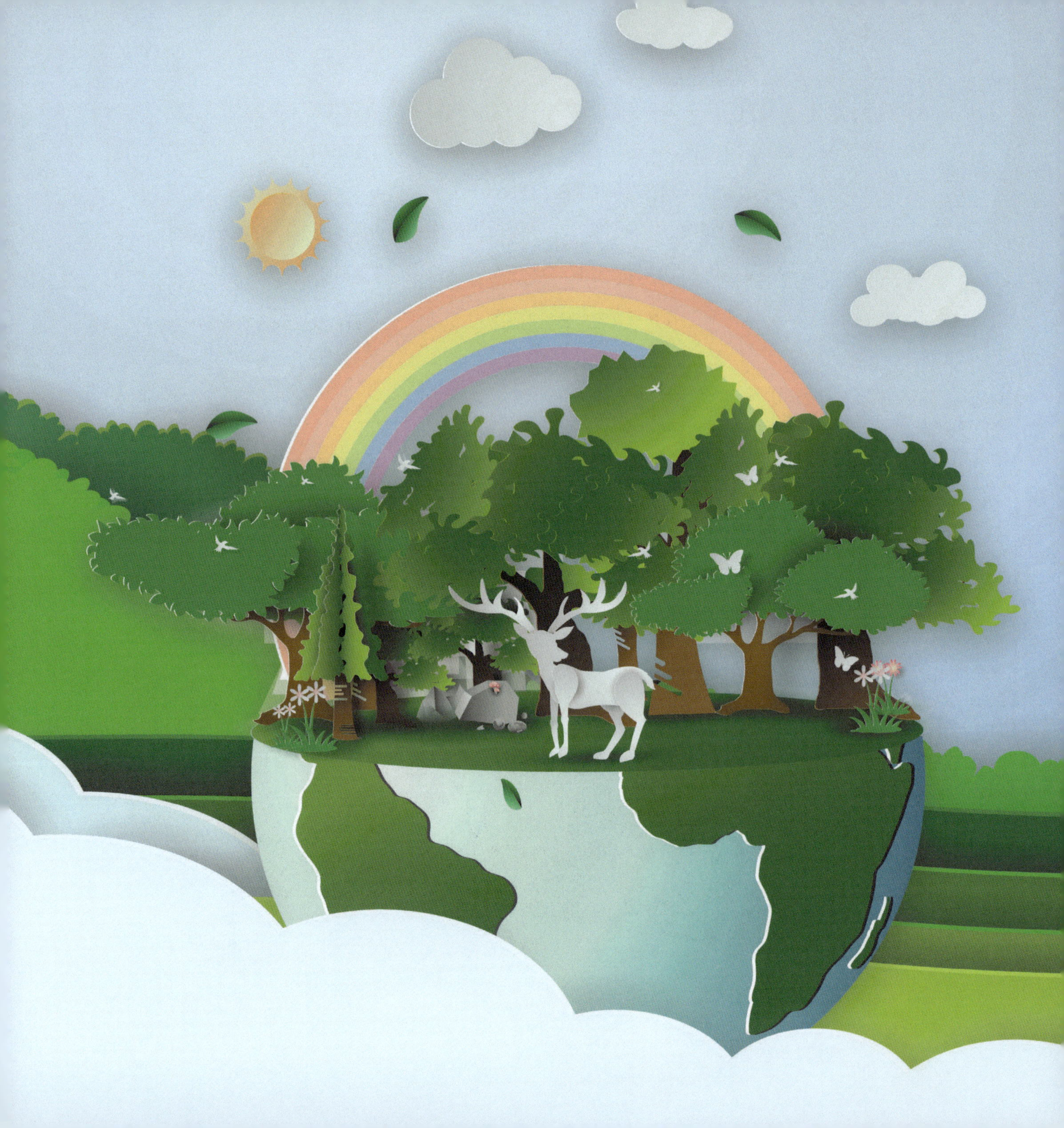

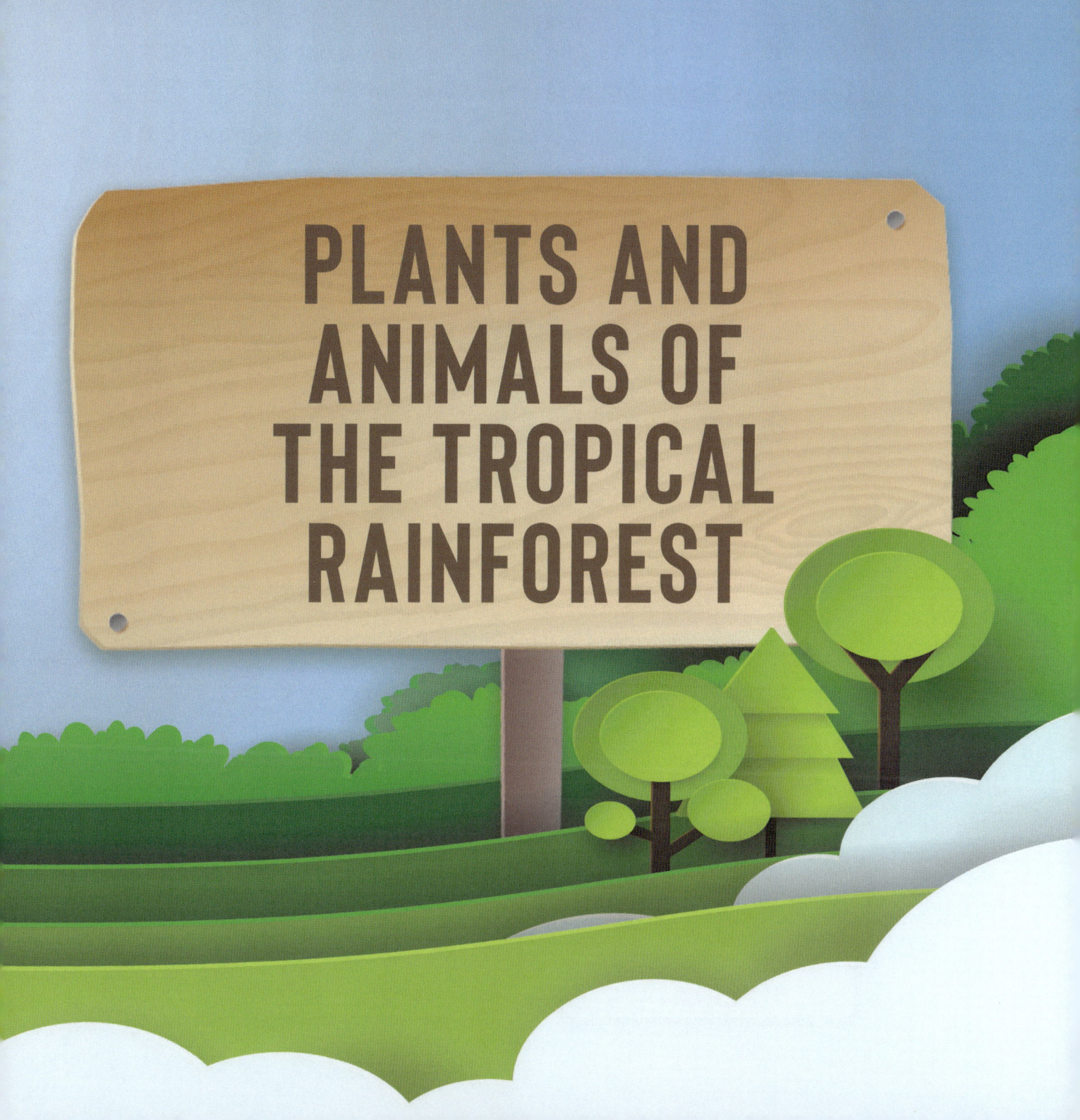

PLANTS AND ANIMALS OF THE TROPICAL RAINFOREST

The diversity of plants and animals in the tropical rainforest biome is staggering. In fact, roughly half of all the world's plant and animal species are found in this biome alone. In the tropical rainforest, you will find rubber trees, banana trees, wild orchids, cacao trees, and coffee plants.

RUBBER TREES

BANANA TREES

WILD ORCHIDS

CACAO TREES

COFFEE PLANTS

The trees grow tall and form an interconnected canopy that is home to hundreds of species of birds. Closer to the ground, you will find monkeys, jaguars, snakes, lizards, sloths, lemurs, and wild boars. Thousands of insect species are also found in the tropical rainforest biomes across the globe.

MONKEYS

SNAKE

JAGUAR

LIZARD

WILD BOAR

LEMURS

SLOTH

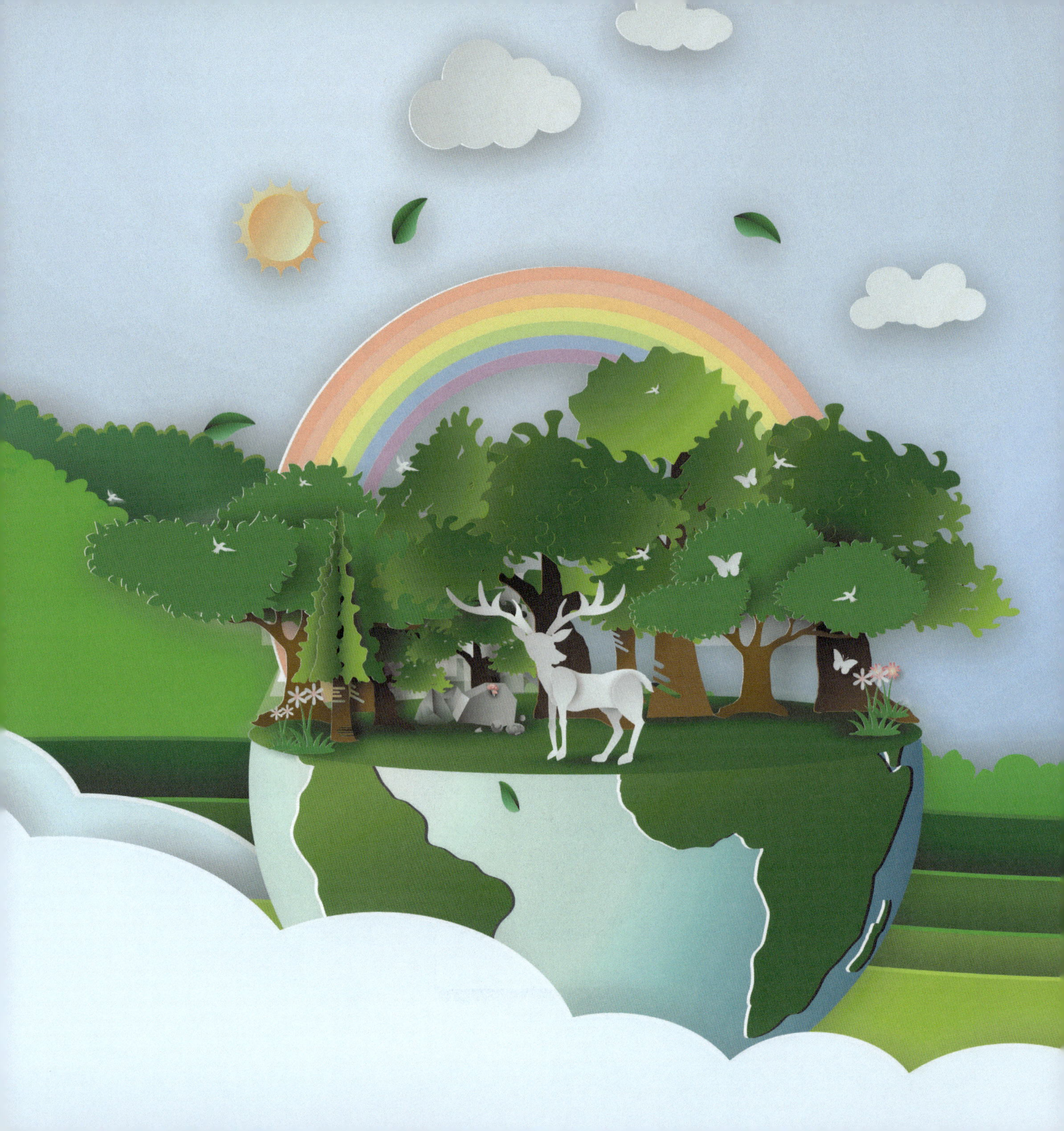

THE GRASSLAND BIOME

As the name suggests, grassland biomes are categorized by an abundance of grass species and very few trees. The Great Plains of the United States and the vast prairies of Canada are grassland biomes.

CANADIAN PRAIRIES

You can also find grasslands in Argentina, Australia, and Russia, to name a few places. Grassland biome experience dry periods, often lasting a long time, that make it unsuitable for the growth of large trees. The grasses in this biome have adapted to the dry spells—they have very long roots that go deep into the soil in search of water.

THE GRASSES IN THIS BIOME HAVE VERY LONG ROOTS THAT GO DEEP INTO THE SOIL IN SEARCH OF WATER.

The dry periods mean that grassland biomes are prone to wildfires, but these fires are beneficial to the habitat. They clear out the dead grasses and add nutrients to the soil. Grassland biomes have some of the richest soil in the world, which is why many grassland biomes have been destroyed to make way for largescale farming.

A SMOKE PLUME OF THE RHEA WILDFIRE AS IT BURNS ACROSS GRASSLANDS IN WESTERN OKLAHOMA.

PLANTS AND ANIMALS OF THE GRASSLAND

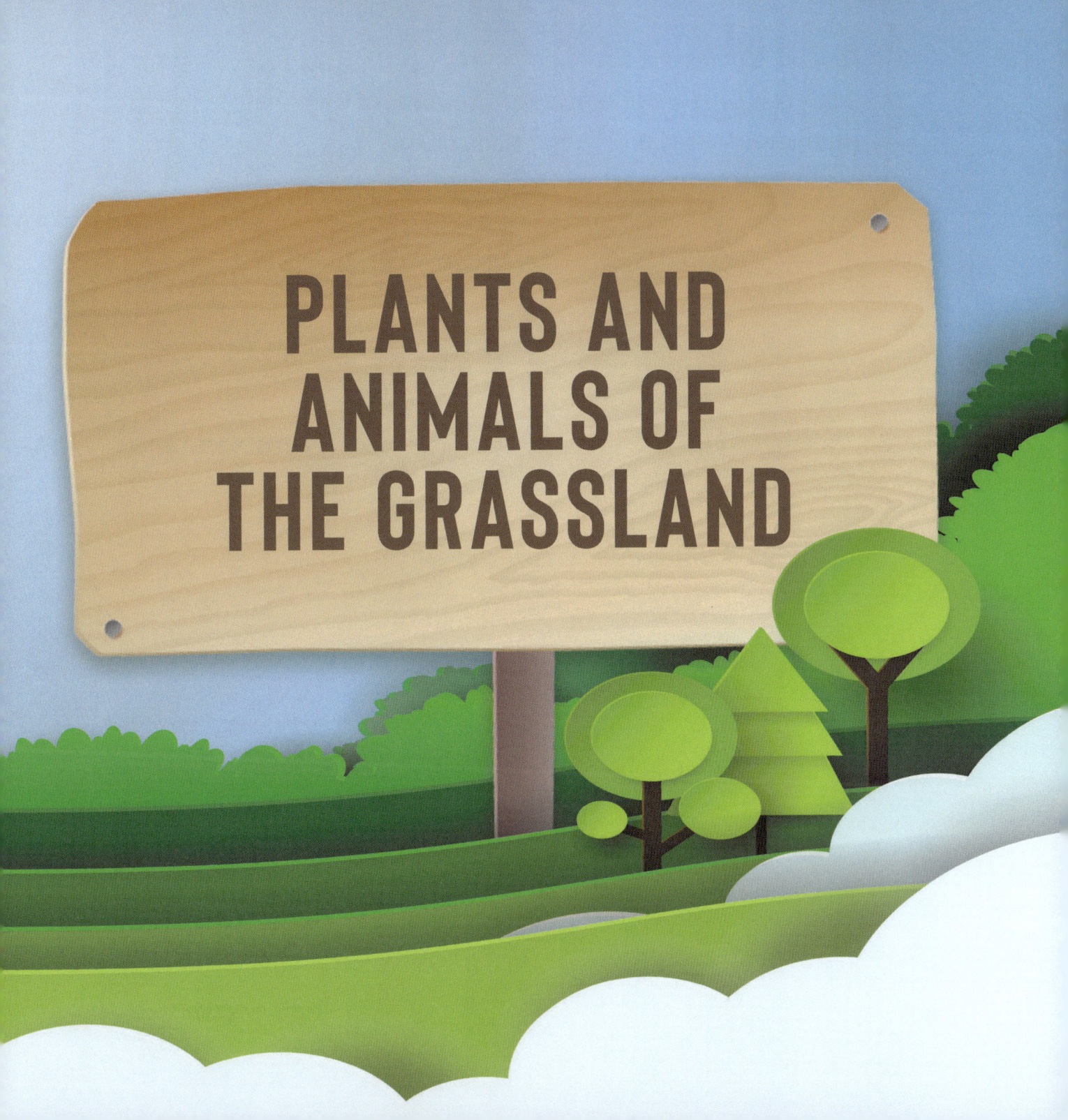

Grassland biomes are ideal for grass plants, like big bluestem, switch grass, and timothy grass. You will also find a wide variety of wildflowers growing in a grassland biome.

BIG BLUESTEM

SWITCH GRASS

TIMOTHY GRASS

Sunflowers, daisies, purple coneflowers, black-eyed Susans, lilies, clover, and asters are common in grasslands.

SUNFLOWERS

PURPLE CORNFLOWERS

DAISIES

BLACK-EYED SUSANS

CLOVERS

LILIES

ASTERS

The grasses and flowers provide food for herds of large, grazing mammals, such as zebras and giraffes in Africa, and buffalo and deer in North America. Birds, insects, and snakes also make their home here.

ZEBRAS AND GIRAFFES

BUFFALO AND DEER

There are, of course, predators that hunt the birds and mammals, for example, wolves, coyotes, and eagles in North America, and big cat species in Africa.

WOLF

COYOTE

EAGLES

BIG CAT

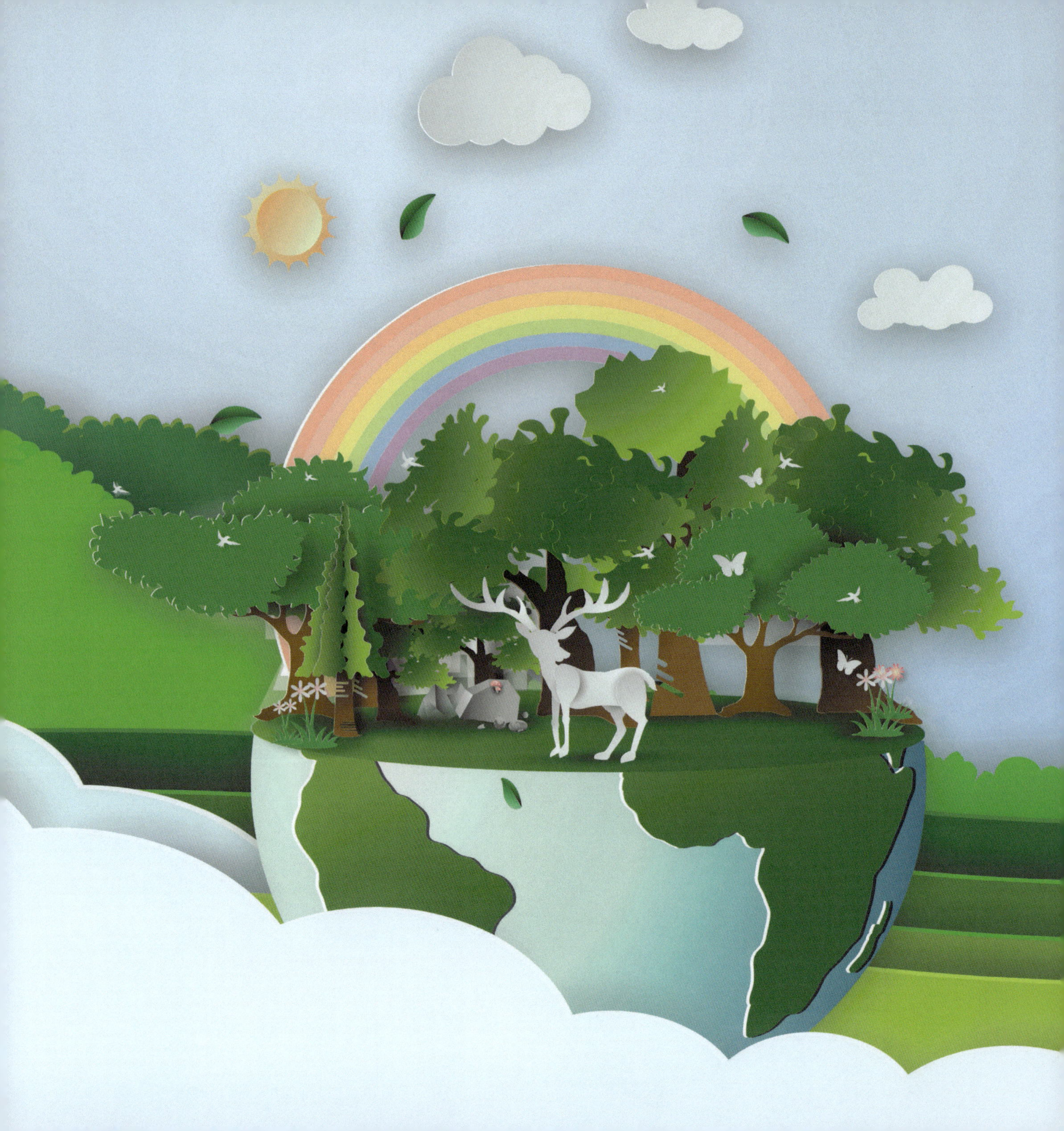

THE TUNDRA BIOME

The coldest biome on Earth is the tundra biome. It is identified by its cold temperatures and lack of trees. Many tundra areas are covered by permanent ice and snow. Others have exposed soil that can support the growth of low-lying grasses, moss, and lichen, however if you dig down a few inches, you will find that the ground is permanently frozen. This is known as the permafrost layer.

TUNDRA BIOME LANDSCAPE IN NORWAY

Tundra biomes are found surrounding the North Pole, in northern Canada, Scandinavia, Russia, Greenland, Iceland, and in the U.S. state of Alaska. You may assume that Antarctica at the South Pole is also a tundra, but the climate and geography is very different there. It is technically considered an arctic desert because of its lack of precipitation. Temperatures in the tundra range from about 55-degrees in the Summer to 30-degrees below zero in the Winter. Annually, the biome experiences about 10 to 12 inches of precipitation.

GLACIER AT PARADISE HARBOR, ANTARCTICA

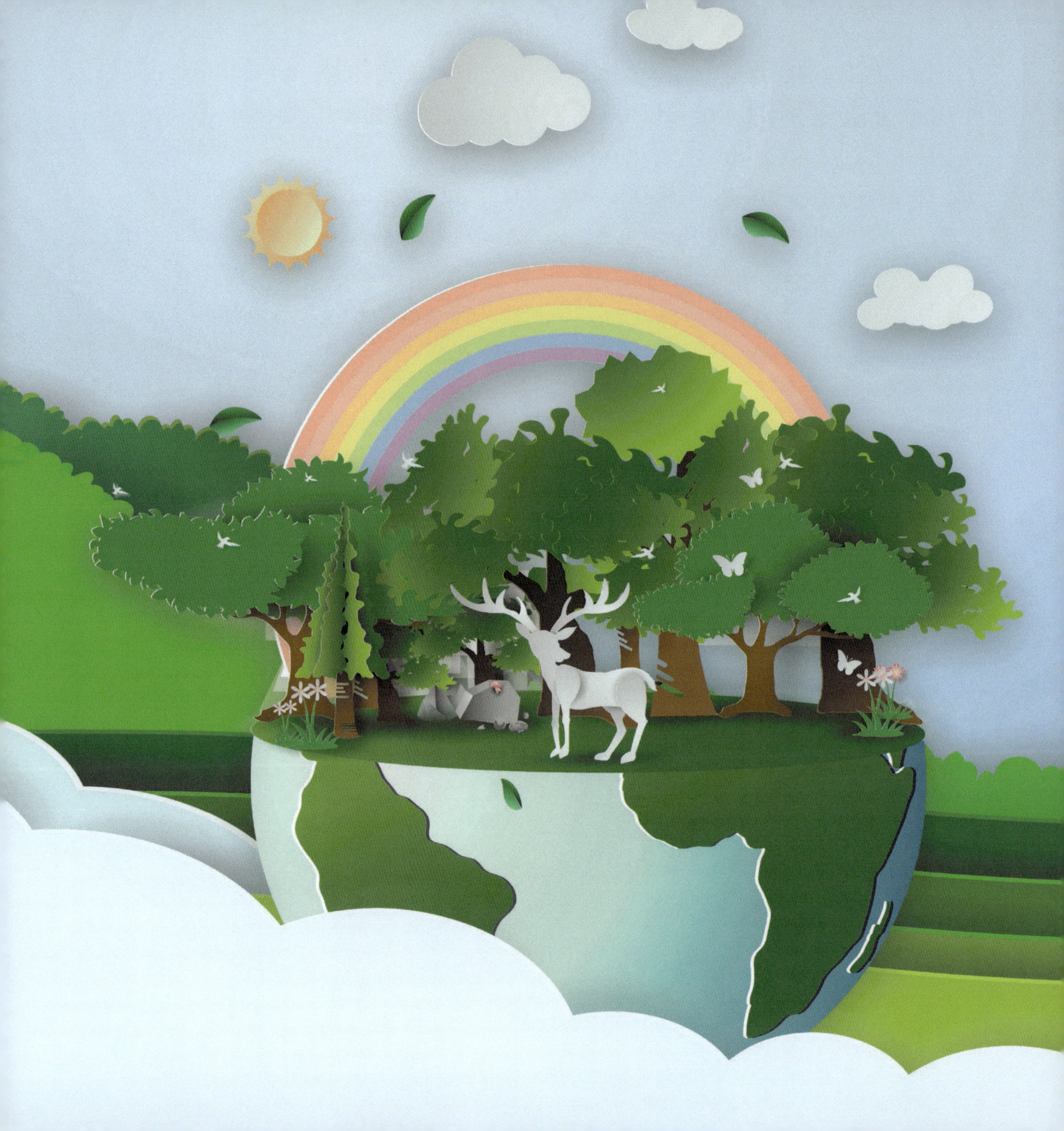

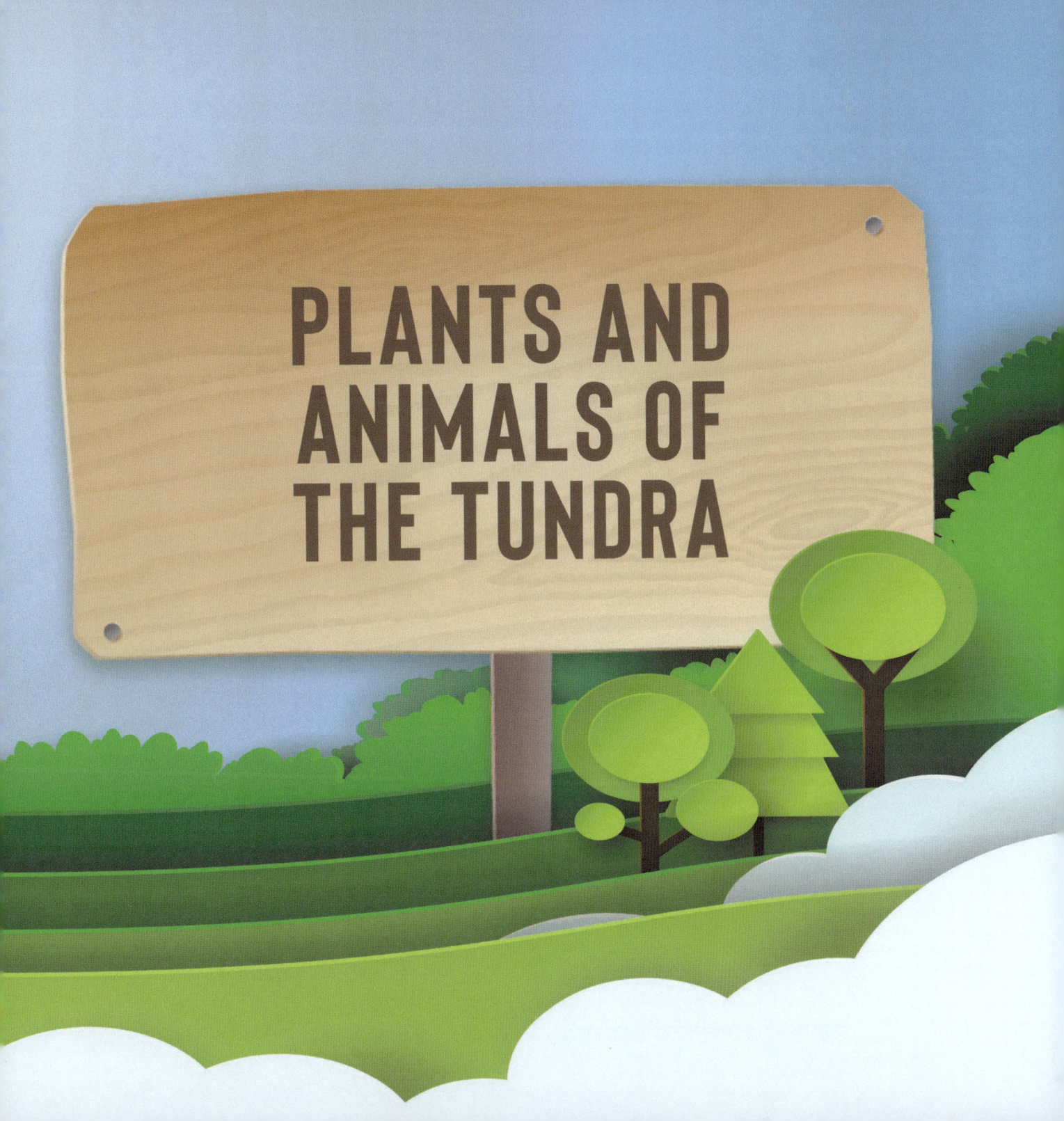

PLANTS AND ANIMALS OF THE TUNDRA

The thin soil, permafrost, cold temperatures, and little rainfall make it difficult for many plants to thrive in the tundra biome. There are, however, several hardy plants that call the tundra their home. They include some varieties of grasses, mosses, low shrubs, sedges, and lichens. Most of these plants take full advantage of the short Summers and experience quick growth spurts during this time.

HARDY PLANTS, LICHEN AND MOSS ON THE TUNDRA OF THE HARDANGER PLATEAU IN NORWAY

Like the plants, the animals of the tundra have adapted to their surroundings. You will find many animals that are white in color, so they blend into the snowy landscapes. These include foxes, hares, polar bears, lemmings, and snowy owls. In addition, the tundra is home to caribou and reindeer herds, as well as migratory birds.

FOX

HARE

POLAR BEAR

LEMMING

SNOWY OWL

CARIBOU

HERD OF REINDEER

MIGRATORY BIRDS

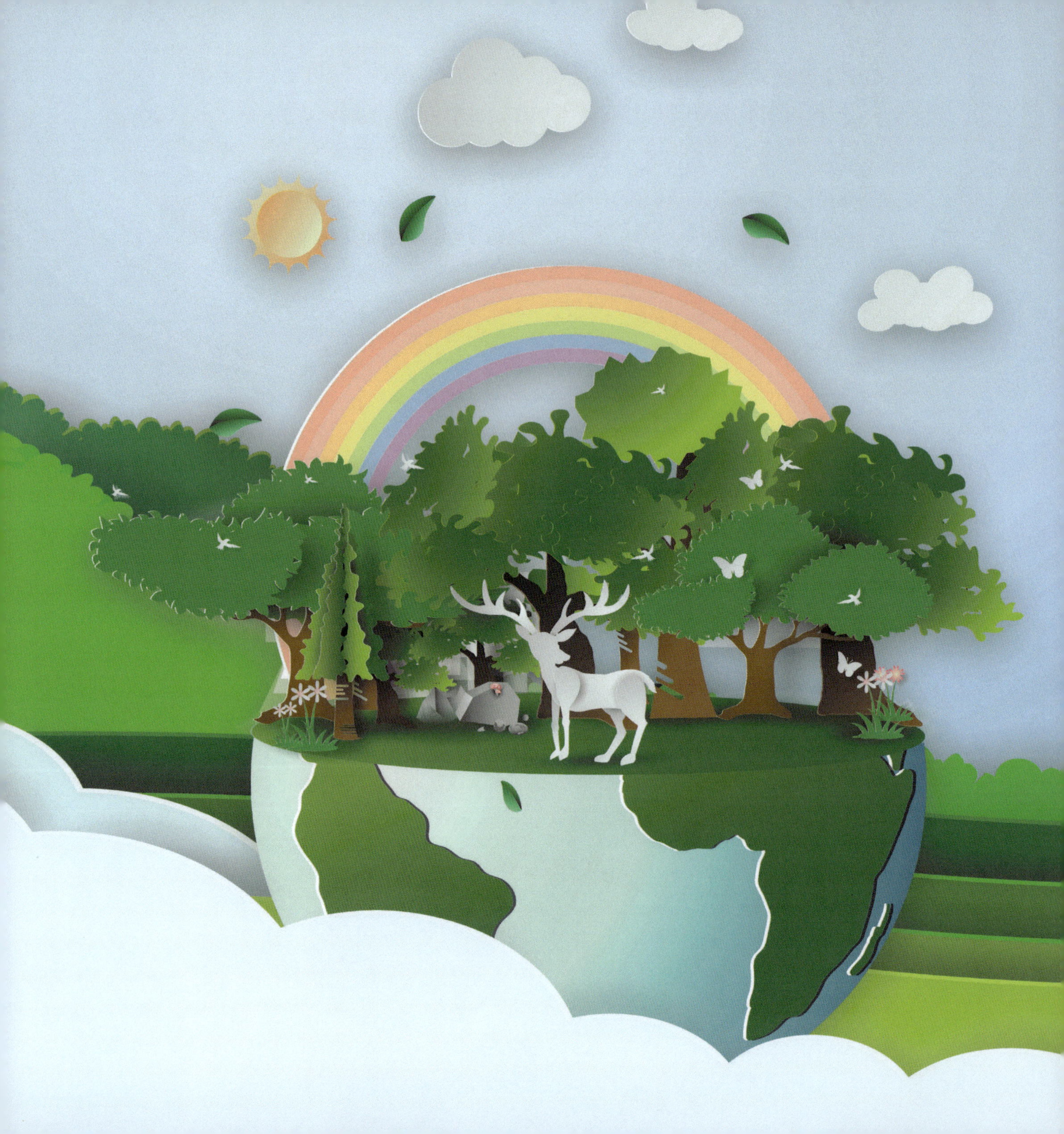

THE SAVANNA BIOME

A savanna is a bit like a grassland except it experiences more annual precipitation. That means, this biome can support the growth of trees, while also sharing some features with grassland biomes. The majority of the savanna biomes on Earth are found in Africa in the areas surrounding the Equator.

AFRICAN SAVANNA

There are, however, savanna biomes located in North and South America, Europe, Asia, and Australia. Like grassland biomes, the savanna biomes go through extended dry periods, but when the rainy season hits, the savanna sees a lot more precipitation. The annual rainfall for a savanna biome is around 50 inches of rain.

TARANGIRE NATIONAL PARK IN TANZANIA, EAST AFRICA

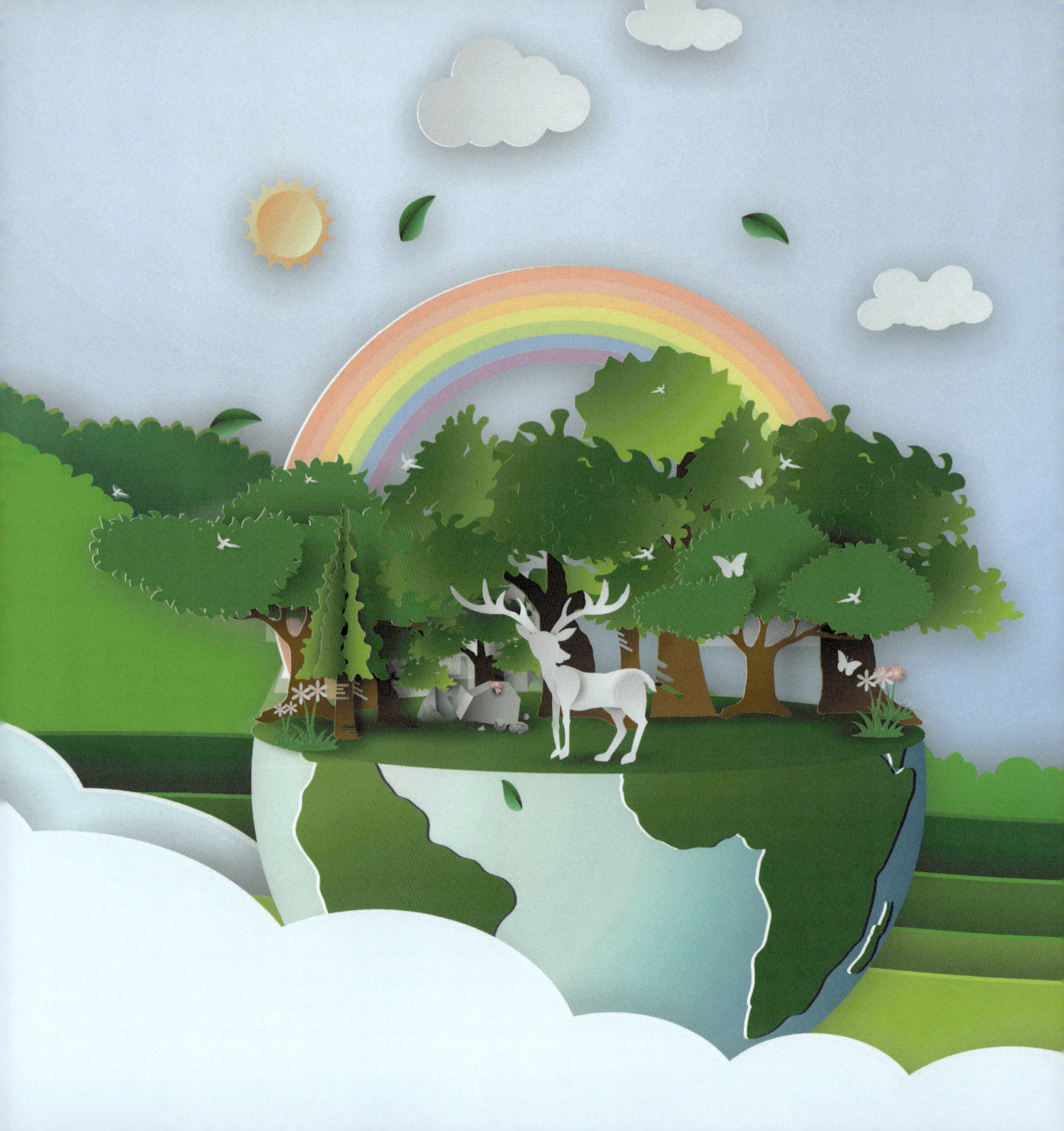

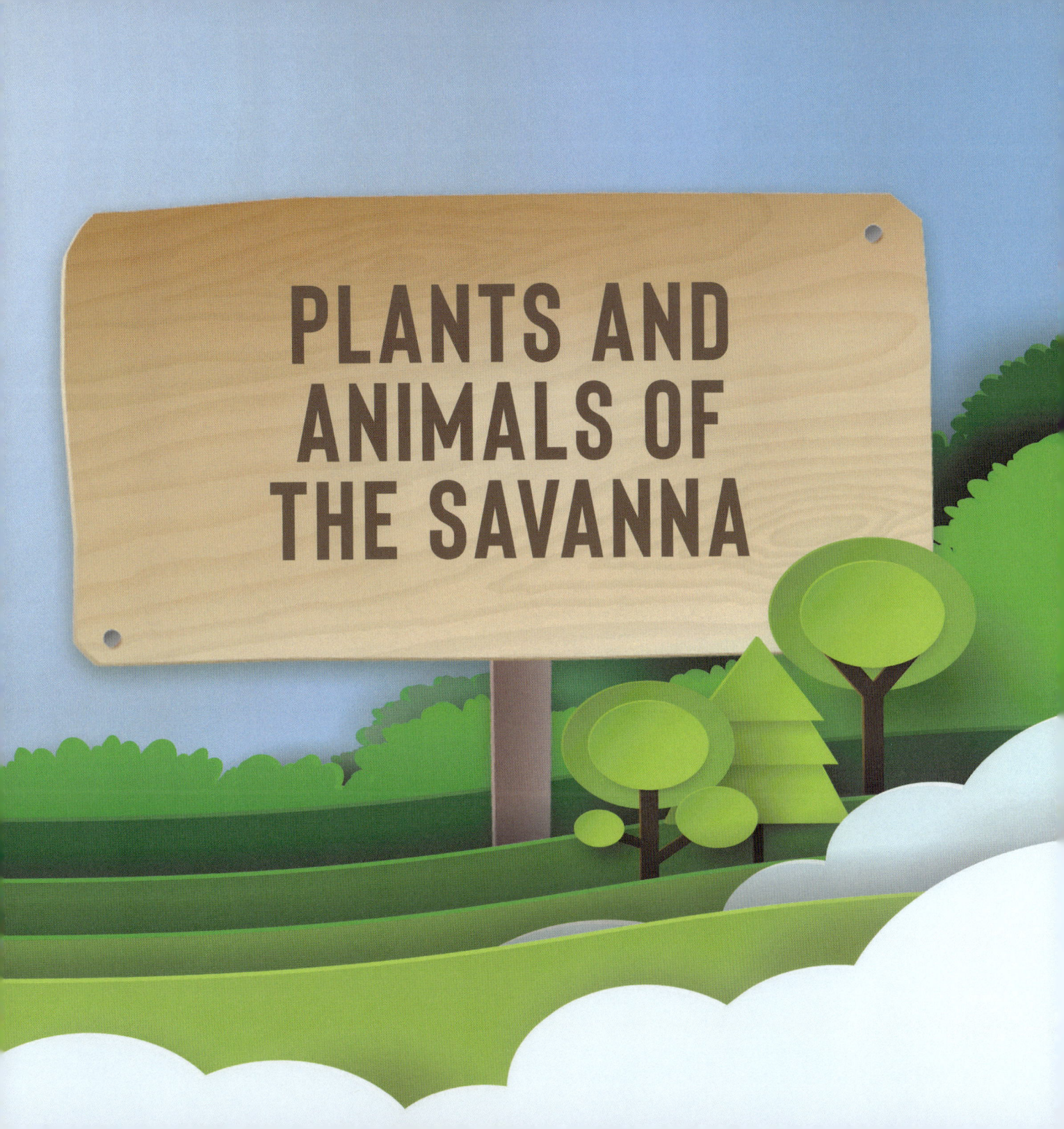

PLANTS AND ANIMALS OF THE SAVANNA

ACACIA AND BAOBAB TREES

76

Baobab and acacia trees are located in savanna biomes. You will, naturally, find a large variety of grasses in this region, as well as shrubs and bushes. This vegetation provides food and cover for the animals of the savanna.

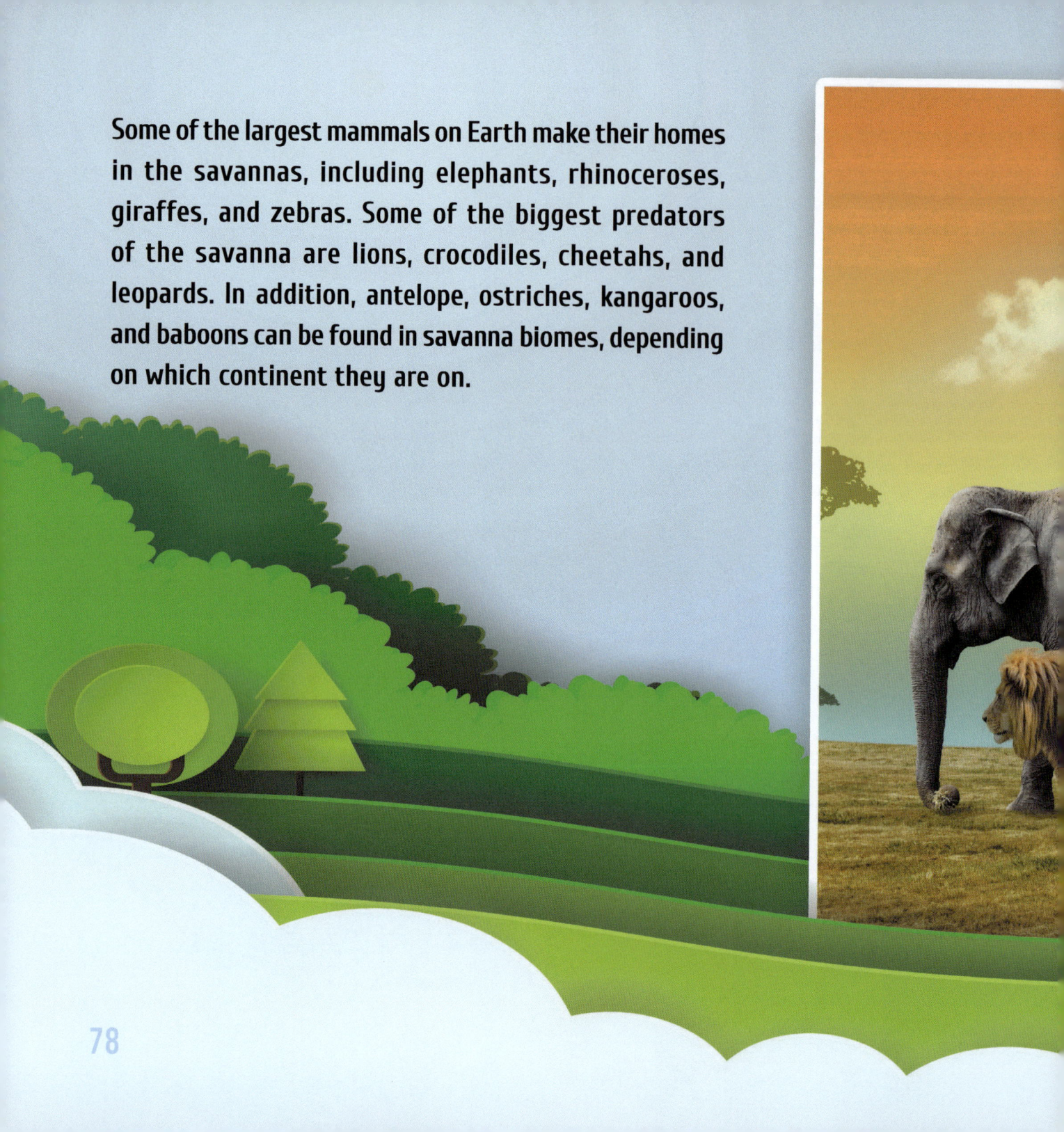

Some of the largest mammals on Earth make their homes in the savannas, including elephants, rhinoceroses, giraffes, and zebras. Some of the biggest predators of the savanna are lions, crocodiles, cheetahs, and leopards. In addition, antelope, ostriches, kangaroos, and baboons can be found in savanna biomes, depending on which continent they are on.

SAVANNA ANIMALS

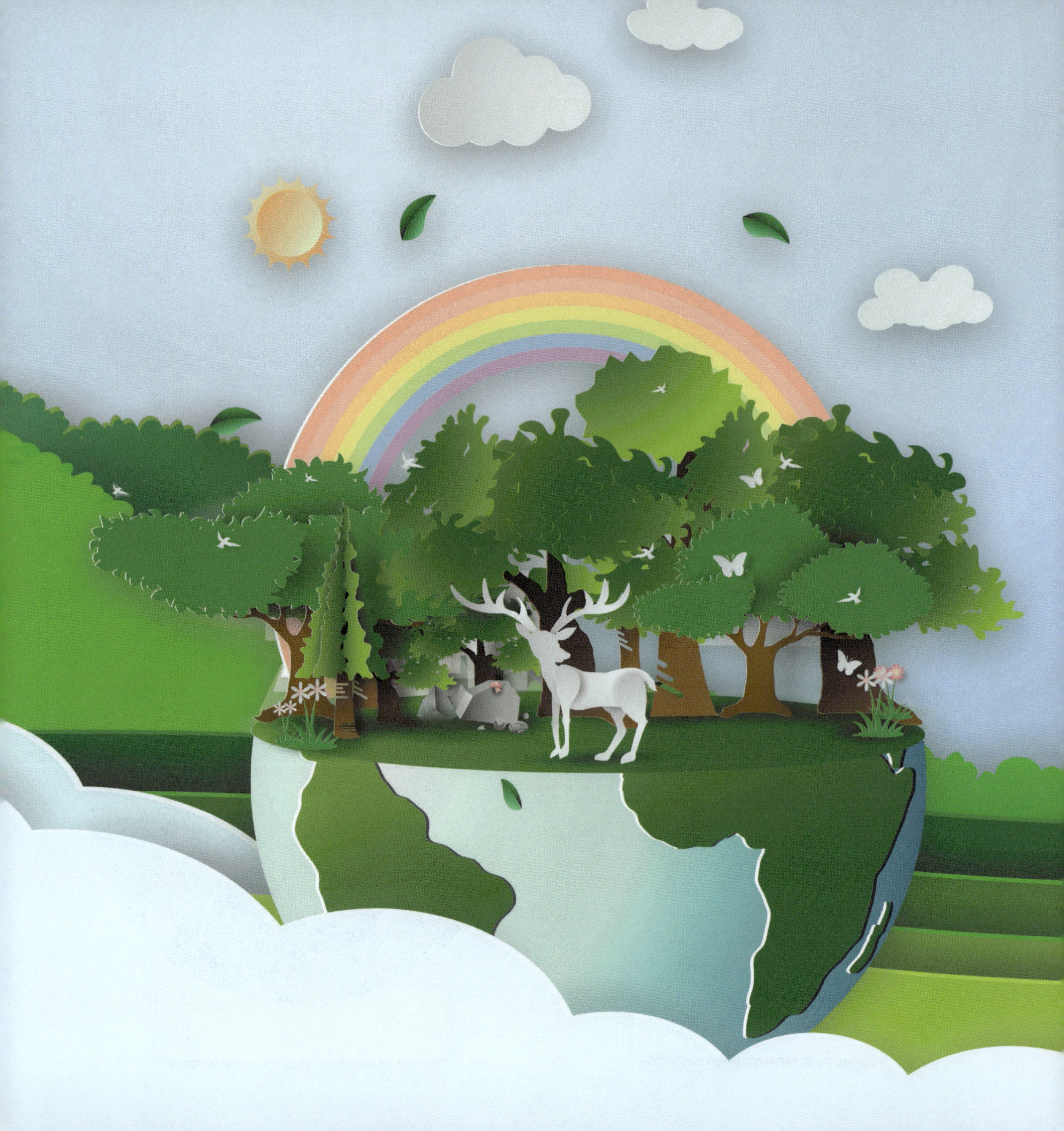

THE TAIGA BIOME

The taiga biome, also called the boreal forest, covers the largest amount of land of any biome. More than a quarter of the planet's landmasses are considered to be boreal forests. This biome is found primarily in the Northern Hemisphere, including Canada, Russia, Europe, and North America.

RIVER FLOWING THROUGH A VALLEY IN BOREAL FOREST, ALASKA, USA

The taiga biome is generally cooler than the temperate forest biome because of its location closer to the Arctic. In the Summertime, the average temperature in the taiga biome hovers around 50-degrees. In the Winter, however, the temperature goes down to about 24-degrees, giving this biome an average annual temperature of about 32-degrees. The taiga biome receive precipitation in the form of rain in the warmer month, with plenty of snow during colder times. The average precipitation is roughly 30-inches each year.

VIEW OF A TAIGA FOREST IN WINTER

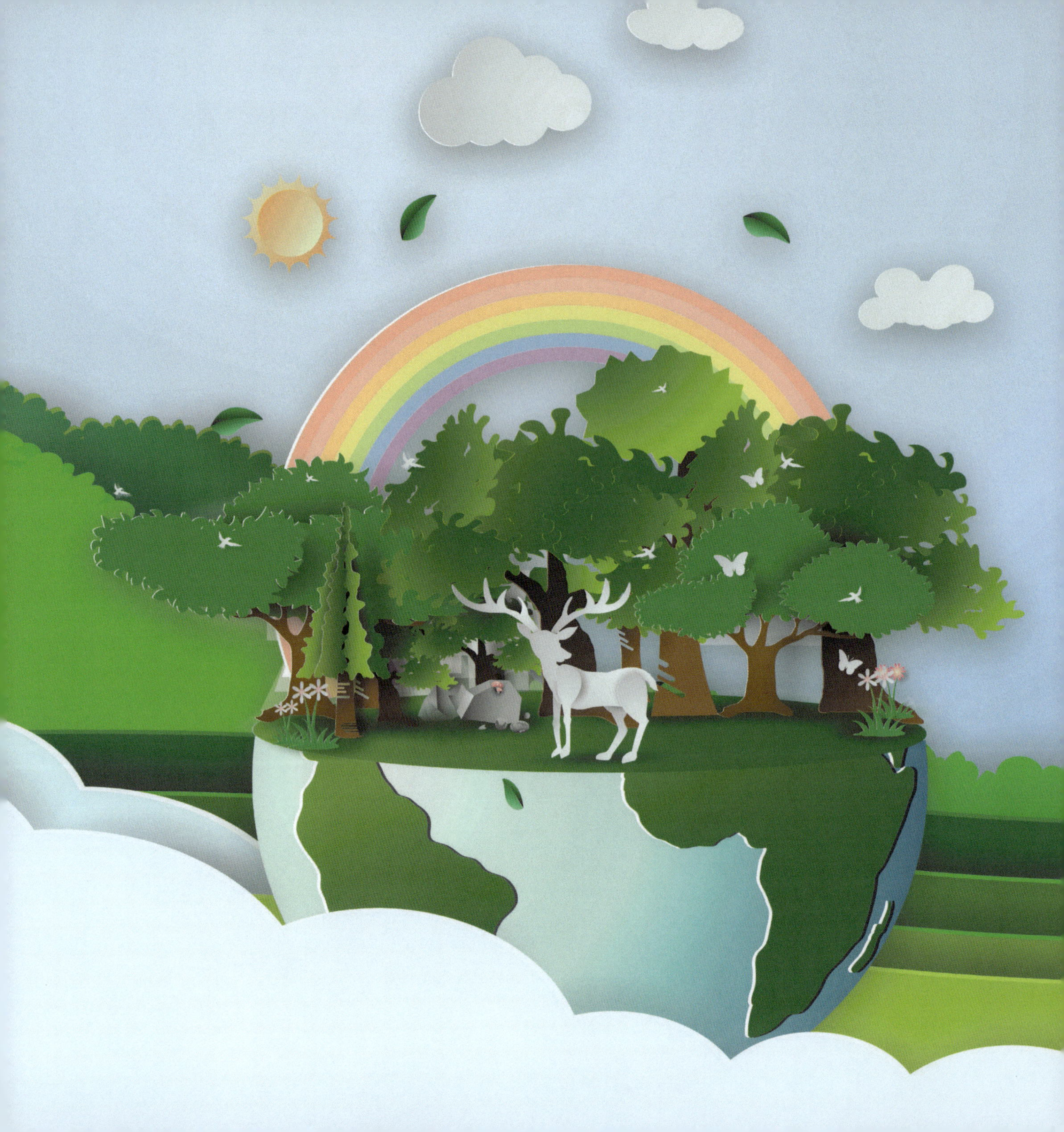

PLANTS AND ANIMALS OF THE TAIGA BIOME

One of the features that sets the taiga biome apart from others is the abundance of evergreen trees in this region. Although there are some deciduous trees, the majority of them are pines, firs, cedars, and spruces. Berry vines, such as blackberries, huckleberries, and raspberries are common, as well as shrubs and wildflowers.

SPRUCE, FIR AND PINE TREES

Many of the animals found in the boreal forest are also native to other biomes. Animals such as deer, moose, caribou, squirrels, eagles, moles, mice, and elk move between different biomes in their search for food and water. A number of the mammals in the taiga will hibernate over the Winter and the birds of this region will migrate to warmer climates until Summer.

| DEER | MOOSE | CARIBOU | SQUIRREL |

| EAGLE | MOLE | MOUSE | ELK |

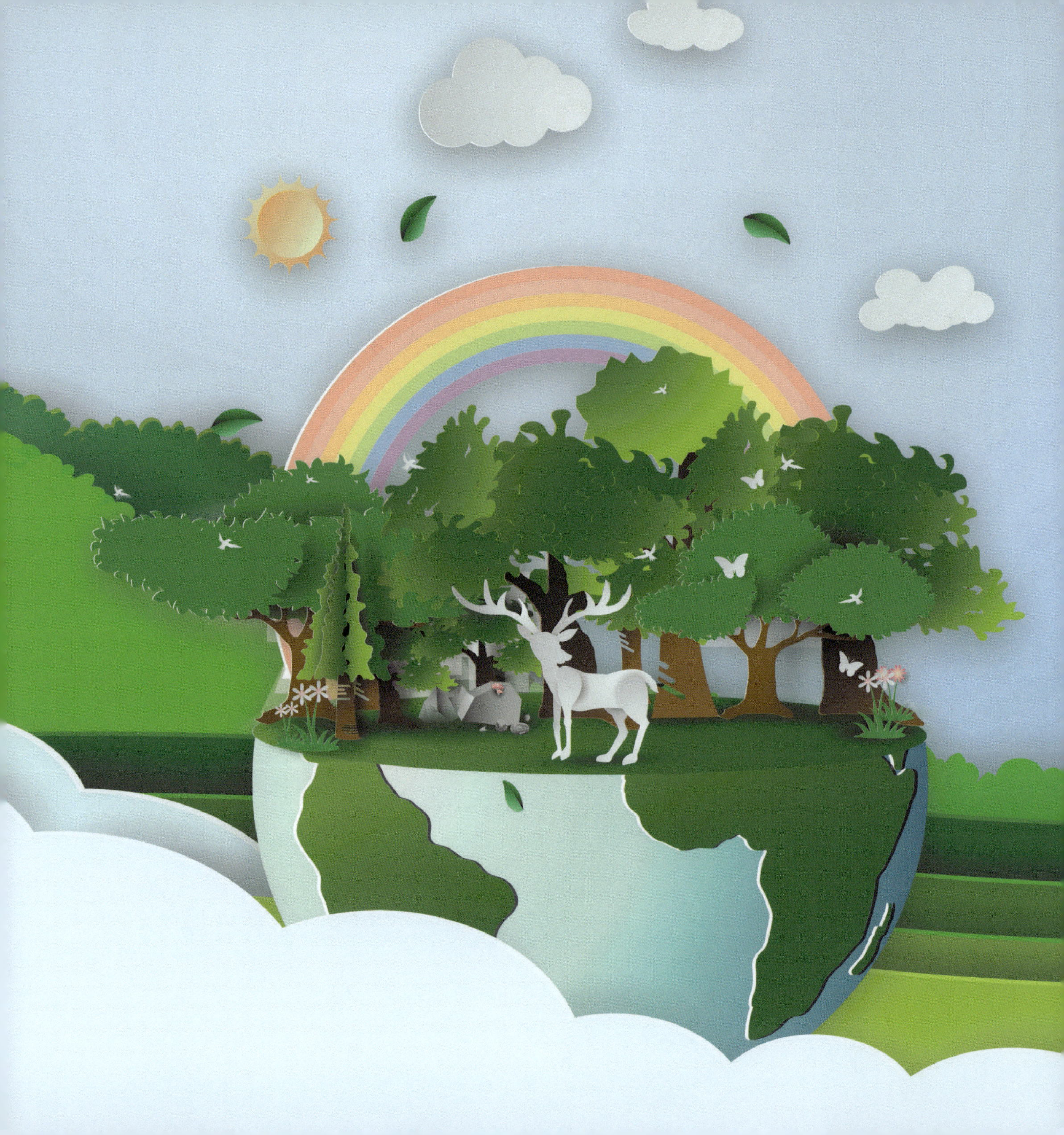

THE FRESHWATER BIOME

Lakes, rivers, streams, estuaries, and ponds make up freshwater biomes. Unlike ocean water, freshwater has a salt content of less than one percent. Although the freshwater can be found in different regions around the world, with vastly different geography and climate, the freshwater biome still offers enough similarities to be considered its own biome. The freshwater biome is often subdivided into different categories to show whether the freshwater biome is located in a tropical or cold climate, or in a grassland or a forested area.

STREAM FLOWING THROUGH WOODS IN TENNESSEE

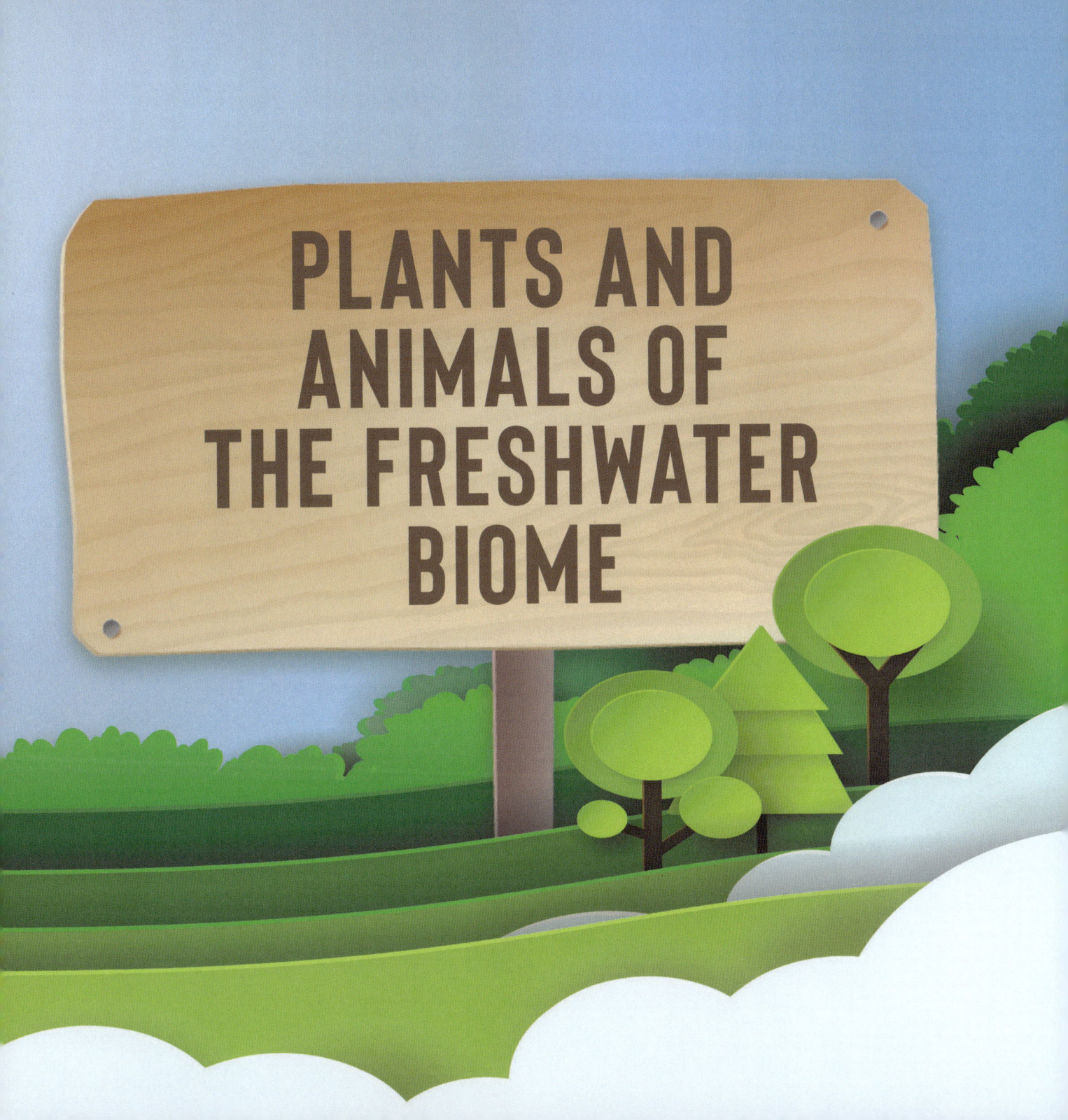

PLANTS AND ANIMALS OF THE FRESHWATER BIOME

The water provides a habitat for numerous plants and animals. Various types of fish are found in freshwater lakes and streams. In addition to fish, you will find insects, snakes, turtles, and birds in freshwater biomes. There are several aquatic mammals, such as mink and beaver, living in freshwater habitats.

SNAKE

TURTLES

BIRDS

MINK

BEAVER

Some plants, like seaweed and lily pads, grow in the water. Others, like reeds, cat-tails, and lilies, grow at the water's edge.

SEAWEEDS

LILY PADS

REEDS

CAT-TAILS

LILIES

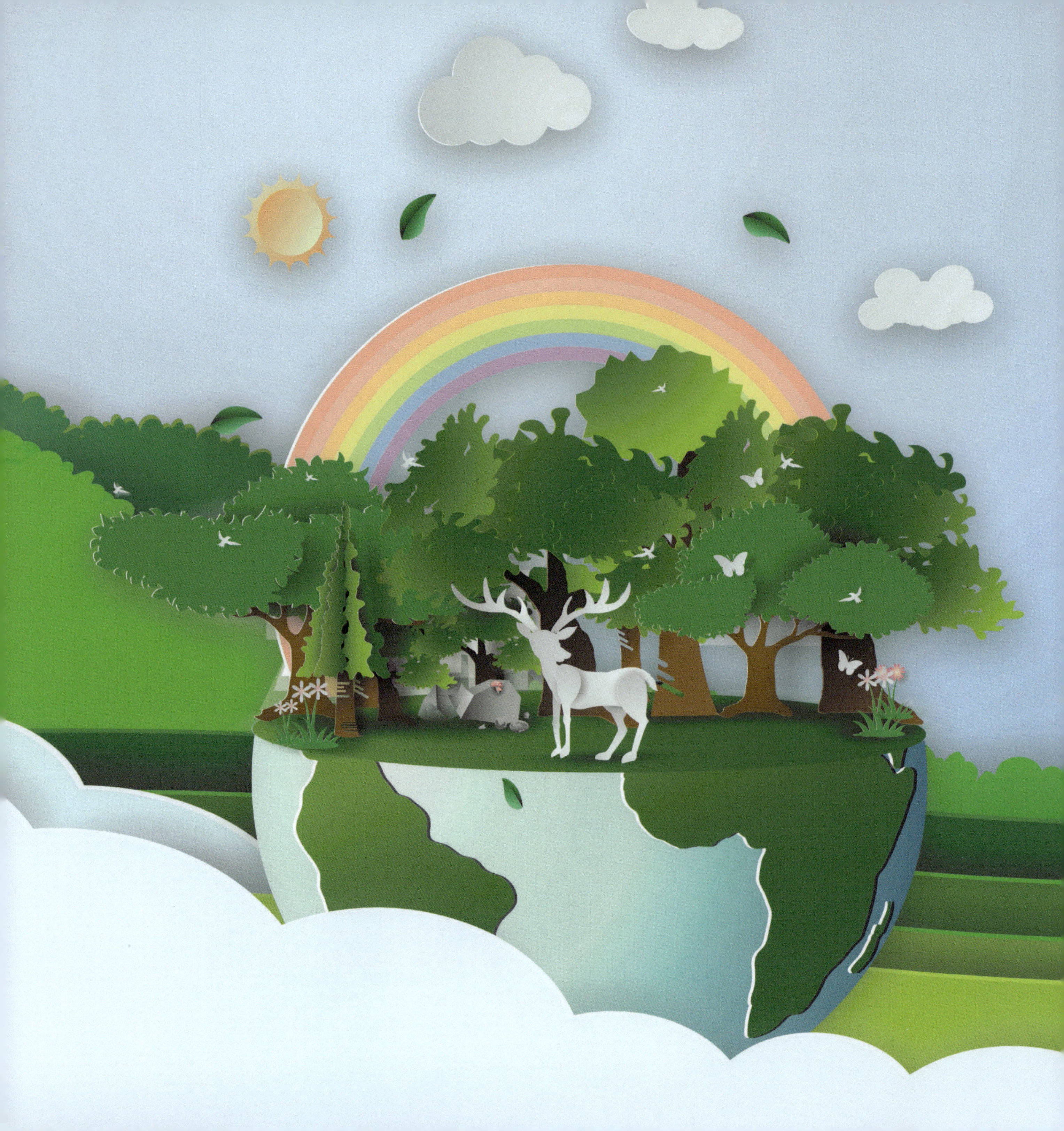

THE MARINE BIOME

The largest aquatic biome is the marine biome, which is comprised of salt water. This includes all the oceans and seas of the world, which is a roughly 70-percent of the planet. Like the freshwater biome, the marine biome is often split into subcategories to reflect different locations and geographical features.

THE LARGEST AQUATIC BIOME IS THE MARINE BIOME.

For example, tide pools are a unique biome, as are coral reefs, deep water trenches, and the ocean floor. In addition, some of the marine biomes are located in tropical areas with warm, balmy temperatures and some are in frigid Arctic climates.

TIDE POOLS

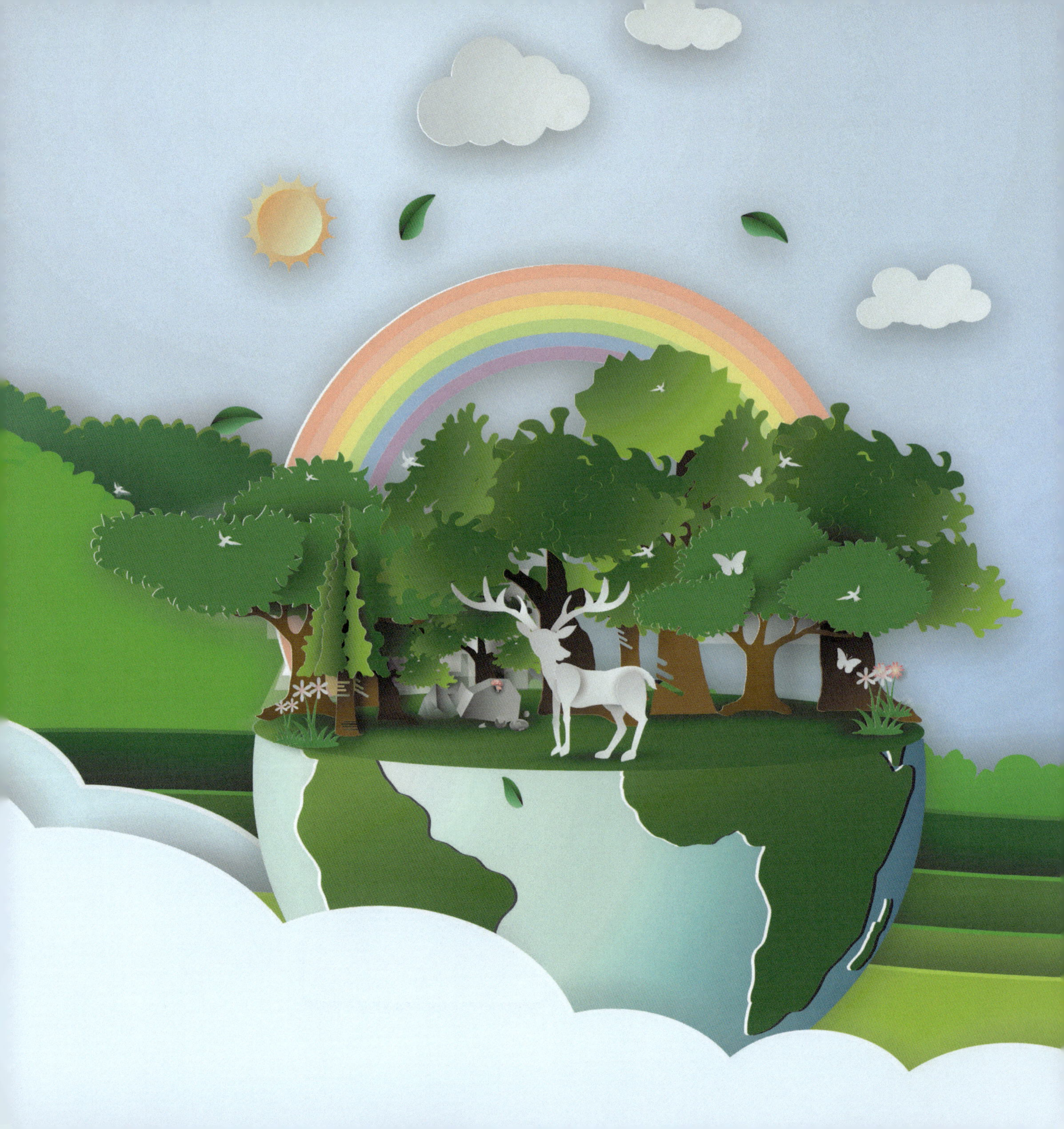

THE PLANTS AND ANIMALS OF THE MARINE BIOME

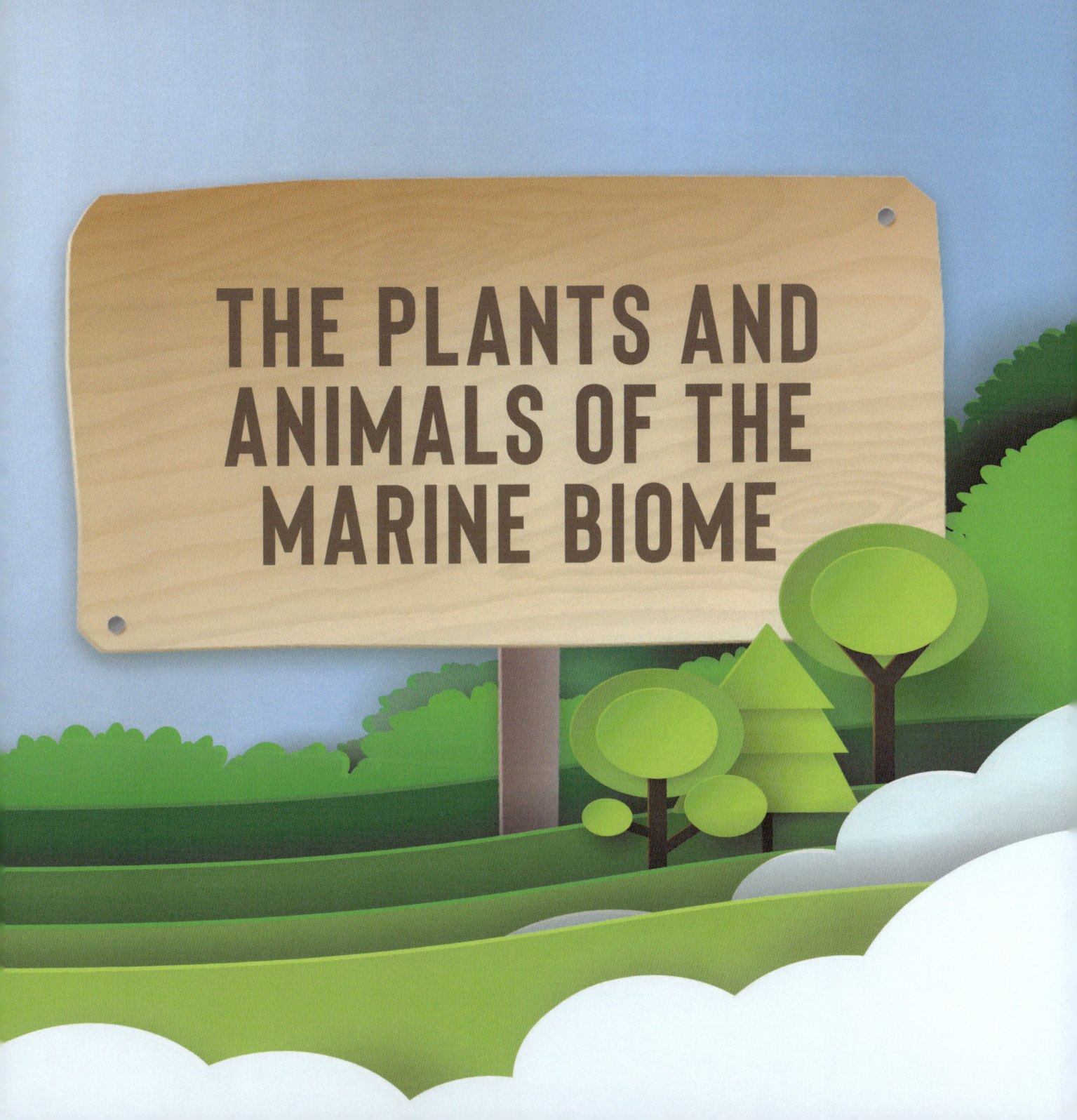

In the oceans and seas of the world, there are plenty of diverse plants, such as seaweed, kelp, and even floating algae. Animal life is even more diverse. Whales are the largest animals on Earth, but the ocean is also home to tiny plankton as well.

ALGAE

KELP

SEAWEEDS

WHALES

PLANKTONS

100

In between, there are mammals, like seals and dolphins; birds, like gulls, osprey, and pelicans; fish like salmon and tuna; crustaceans, like crabs and shrimps; mollusks like octopi and snails; reptiles like sea turtles and sea snakes. The oceans are teeming with life.

SEALS	DOLPHINS	GULLS	OSPREY
SALMON	TUNA	CRABS	SHRIMPS
OCTOPUS	SNAILS	SEA TURTLE	SEA SNAKE

SUMMARY

By grouping together similar habitats in distinct biomes, biologists are better able to study the plants and animals living there. Although there is some debate over the number of biomes on Earth, we focused on nine of them – the temperate forest, desert, tropical rainforest, grassland, tundra, savanna, taiga, freshwater, and marine biomes.

Now that you have a good overview of some of the common biomes, you can delve into one or more of the ones that interest you the most, learning more about the climate, physical features, plants, and animals found there.

Visit

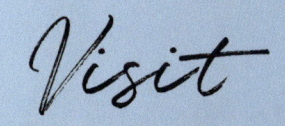

www.speedypublishing.com

To view and download free content on your favorite subject and browse our catalog of new and exciting books for readers of all ages.

Printed in Great Britain
by Amazon